# 100
GREATS

# HAMPSHIRE
## County Cricket Club

Lionel Tennyson (left) and Phil Mead at Portsmouth around 1925.

# 100 GREATS

# HAMPSHIRE

## COUNTY CRICKET CLUB

COMPILED BY
NEIL JENKINSON, DAVE ALLEN & BILL RICQUIER

TEMPUS

**Key:**

The letters at the top of the page refer to the following batting or bowling styles:

RHB – right-handed batsman
LHB – left-handed batsman
OB – off-spinner
ROB – right-handed off-break bowler
SLA – slow left arm spin
RF – right-handed fast
RFM – right-arm fast medium
RSM – right-arm slow medium
LFM – left-arm fast medium
RM – right-arm medium pace
RLB – leg break bowler
WKT – wicketkeeper
Lobs – bowled under-arm

First published 2003

Tempus Publishing Limited
The Mill, Brimscombe Port,
Stroud, Gloucestershire, GL5 2QG

British Library Cataloguing in Publication Data.
A catalogue record for this book is available from the British Library.

ISBN 0 7524 2188 3

Typesetting and origination by Tempus Publishing Limited
Printed in Great Britain by Midway Colour Print, Wiltshire

# Introduction

This book does not claim to offer *the* definitive list of Hampshire's greatest 100 cricketers. In many cases there will be no dispute about the players chosen, but others will be less familiar and it is to be hoped that some inclusions and omissions will encourage lively debate.

This is not the first attempt to go some way towards defining such a list. Most recently, an edition of Hampshire's newsletter to members (no. 21, 2/2000) proposed a list of Hampshire's greatest eleven cricketers – not chosen to form a side but for outstanding individual achievement. The main criterion was 100 first-class appearances, which excluded such great players as C.B. Fry, Gower, Roberts and Warne. The proposed eleven had – entirely by chance – the look of a well-balanced side and they would clearly be formidable opponents: Richards, Greenidge, R.E. Marshall, Mead, R. Smith, Brown, Sainsbury, Kennedy, M.D. Marshall, Newman and Shackleton. If such a side were to take the field, Brown would keep wicket and the last five would probably capture a few wickets – indeed the captain's main problem might be who would share the new ball with Marshall? The selectors' main concern would be who to choose as captains. The second XI would be more than useful and might comprise: Gray, C.L. Smith, R.M. Poore, Jesty, A.J.L. Hill, Rogers, Leo Harrison, Tremlett, Cottam, White and Knott. Neville Rogers, who had a brief but outstanding experience as a captain, might lead that side. Even then, there is no place for the double international Johnny Arnold, Henry Horton, Paul Terry, David Turner or the captains Tennyson, Ingleby-Mackenzie, Gilliat and Nicholas. We might wish to include Neil McCorkell, Bob Parks and Adie Aymes but cannot displace Leo and we must apologise to bowlers as fine as Harry Baldwin and Stuart Boyes for their omission. If the side were ever short of fun we might call upon Jim Bailey and 'Lofty' Herman and with sadness we might wonder about the potential of Arthur Jacques or Donald Walker had they not been called to sacrifice in a fiercer contest.

Warming to the task, we might seek to assemble a side of recruits with appearances for other counties. In such a side, Mike Taylor, Kevan James, Vic Cannings, Bob Herman, Raj Maru, Peter Hartley and Alan Mullally would trouble many good batsmen and Bob Stephenson would keep wicket, but we might need to relax our appearances rule and call upon C.B. Fry, Crawley and Gower to support the batting of Cliff Walker. A side of overseas internationals could begin with C.B. Llewellyn, 'cheat' by including R.M. Poore and prosper with men like Richards, Greenidge, Hayden, Johnson, the two Marshalls, Roberts and Warne, but who would keep wicket to such an attack? Perhaps Pothas qualifies? Many counties would claim that their best elevens could compete with Hampshire's but can any county claim an overseas XI to match this (with reserves including Heath Streak, who bowled tirelessly in 1995, Livingstone, Creese, and O'Sullivan)?

By contrast, a Hampshire-born XI might select from many of the above including Gray, Jesty, Bailey, Sainsbury, wicketkeepers Aymes, Harrison or McCorkell, Cannings, Newman, Boyes, and Knott. To that squad we would add Stone, Wassell, Barnard, Malcolm Heath, Burden, Udal, Chris Tremlett, Kenway and, in particular, Tony Middleton, whose career average of 34.75 is higher than any other native batsman.

If we were to send such sides into the field, allowing for Tremlett and Sainsbury as players, the choice of coach would be simple: Arthur Holt who would bring joy, kindness and wisdom to his task. John Arlott would handle all broadcasts and newspaper reports while Harry Altham would provide the historical context, assisted by Desmond Eagar who would also manage procedures. Vic Isaacs would score and compile statistics in written *and* virtual form while Ernie Knights and Nigel Gray would share responsibility for the grounds, allowing each the opportunity of a well-earned rest and cup of tea.

The list of players above numbers seventy, so we approach the first hundred with little effort and hardly any consideration of the greatest innovation of the past forty years, limited-overs cricket. Were we to take this into account, many of the players above would feature and so too would Cardigan Connor and Jon Ayling (who played in all three finals), Steven Jefferies for his great day at Hampshire's first Lord's final in 1988, Nigel Cowley, and John Rice. As we move beyond these names and often back into the very early days of Hampshire cricket, the debates will increase. We have not, for example, yet mentioned Barton, Heseltine and Wynyard (who all represented England), nor our two top-scorers, Sir Francis Lacey and Dick Moore. Other sterling performers to miss out include Mike Barnard, Alan Rayment, Denis Baldry, Barry Reed, Tom Mottram, John Southern, Keith Stevenson and Peter Hartley. John Stephenson will no doubt find a home in *100 Essex Greats*.

Another difficulty in defining such a list is giving adequate consideration to the potential of Hampshire's younger cricketers. We have included only Mascarenhas and Kendall from Hampshire's cricketers under the age of thirty, but there is undoubted promise elsewhere and it is quite possible – and indeed to be hoped – that a revision of this book in 2010 might see some or even all of the following names included: Derek Kenway, Chris Tremlett, Lawrence Prittipaul, James Tomlinson, James Schofield and James Hamblin. Almost certainly, John Crawley would warrant inclusion by then for, as we complete our efforts during the summer of 2002, his first weeks for his new county have re-established him as an England cricketer. In addition, we have no way of knowing who might appear in the side over the next decade but if the list does require significant revision one hopes that this might signify years of success on the field to match their growing ambitions off it.

The writing of this book has given us great pleasure, not least in its opportunity to honour those men who have brought us similar pleasure (and the occasional frustration) over the years. It is a testimony to the history of Hampshire County Cricket Club at that moment when, publicly it re-presents itself as Hampshire Cricket. It is entering an exciting but difficult new period and we must hope that the future supporters of Hampshire Cricket can look forward to seeing as many exciting players in the future as we have been privileged to write about here.

## Acknowledgements

Colin Ingleby-Mackenzie for the foreword. Vic Isaacs for the statistics. Andrew Renshaw, Fr. Felix Stephens OSB, Jean M. Jones, Sahlawati Kassim, Steve Eason, Malcolm Merry, John May MPS.

## Bibliography

Cricket: A Weekly Record
Wisden Cricketer's Almanack
Benson and Hedges Cricket Year
Hamphire Handbook
Wisden Cricket Monthly
Christopher Martin-Jenkins, World Cricketers: A Bibliographical Dictionary
    (Oxford University Press, 1996)
Peter Wynne-Thomas, The History of Hampshire County Cricket Club (Christopher Helm, 1998)
P.J. Bailey, P.R. Thorn and P. Wynne-Thomas, Who's Who of Cricketers
Chris Westcott, Class of '59 (Mainstream Publishing, 2000)
A.A. Thomson, Vintage Ellvans (Pelham Books, 1969)
John Arlott, Cricket in the Counties (Saturn Press, 1950)
John Arlott, The Australian Challenge (William Heinemann, 1961)

Arlott on Cricket, ed. David Rayvern Allen (Willow Books, 1984)
Michael Marshall, Gentlemen and Players (Grafton Books, 1987)
The Innings of My Life, compiled by Jack Bannister (Headline Book Publishing, 1993)
Mihir Bose, Cricket Voices (The Kingswood, 1990)
Michael Manley, A History of West Indies Cricket (Andre Deutsch, 1988)
Simon Wilde, Letting Rip (H.F. & G. Witherby, 1994)
Roy Marshall, Test Outcast (Pelham Books, 1970)
Barry Richards, The Barry Richards Story (Faber and Faber, 1978)
David Matthews, On the Spot: Derek Shackleton, A Biography
   (Blackberry Downs Books, 1998)

# Historical Note

Hampshire County Cricket Club was formed in 1863, and the comparatively few matches which they played each year until 1885 have been adjudged first class by the Association of Cricket Historians and Statisticians and, as this has been generally accepted, we have followed the adjudication in this book. It is a matter of history that the county's games have been first class since 1895, with the exception of the years 1914-18 and 1939-45.

# Foreword by A.C.D. Ingleby-Mackenzie

Shortly after the end of the Second World War, during my final year at prep school, I arrived at Northlands Road for the first time to be coached in the cricketing basics by some of Hampshire's professionals.

My tutor was the talented and kindly all-rounder Jim Bailey. Somebody thought I showed promise and Harry Altham, player, historian, Test selector and president of the county (and eventually of MCC) was called to judge. He in turn asked for Hampshire's new captain-secretary, Desmond Eagar, who instructed Jim to bowl at me. He delivered a kindly half-volley or two which I managed to despatch correctly and a relationship was formed with the county which I am proud to say survives to this day.

It is delightful to see that the four of us, Harry, Desmond, Jim and I are gathered together again in this book, which I note offers us 100 great players, but wisely and not necessarily *the* 100 greats. That might give us all food for thought.

There are men here that I knew only by reputation, some that I met in their later years, friends and colleagues from my own sides and great players of recent years. Much has been made over the years of Hampshire as a 'happy' club and there are many players here who will remind us of great pleasures and of good fun. This is how cricket should be, for it is a *game* and one best played and watched in good spirits, good company and fine weather.

Nonetheless, there are also great players here whose greatness, by any standards, was a product of skill, craft, determination and hard work. Much has been made over the years of my philosophy of 'wine, women and song' which brought us fresh success in 1961, but what is sometimes forgotten is that the fun we had (and we did!) was built upon the high cricketing standards of my players. And just as I had Roy and Jimmy, 'Shack' and dear Leo; so Lionel Tennyson could turn to his great professionals Phil Mead, George Brown and Kennedy and Newman, and later captains to Richards and Greenidge, Marshall and Roberts, the Smith brothers or Gosport's Trevor Jesty.

They and many others are here to remind us again of great days and great names in Hampshire cricket. I hope their memory will bring you pleasure and that the next generation will, by their exploits, soon be demanding inclusion in any list of great Hampshire cricketers.

# 100 Hampshire Greats

Cecil Halliday Abercrombie
Ronald Aird
Harry Surtees Altham
John Arlott
John Arnold
Jon Ayling
Adrian Aymes
Francis Hugh Bacon
John Badcock
Jim Bailey
Harry Baldwin
Mike Barnard
Victor Alexander Barton
*Sir Russell Bencraft*
Alec Bowell
Stuart Boyes
*George Brown*
Mervyn Burden
Vic Cannings
Cardigan Connor
Bob Cottam
Nigel Cowley
W.L.C. Creese
*Desmond Eagar*
Colonel James Fellows
Charles Burgess Fry
Richard Gilliat
David Gower
Jimmy Gray
*Gordon Greenidge*
Canon John Glennie Greig
Leo Harrison
Matthew Hayden
George Heath

Malcolm Heath
Oswald William Herman
Bob Herman
Col. Christopher Heseltine
Arthur James Ledger Hill
Gerry Hill
Arthur Holt
Henry Horton
*Colin Ingleby-Mackenzie*
Kevan James
Arthur Jaques
Trevor Jesty
Neil Johnson
Colonel A.C. Johnston
Will Kendall
*Alexander S. Kennedy*
C.J. 'Charlie' Knott
Sir Francis Eden Lacey
Danny Livingstone
Walter Livsey
*Charles Bennett Llewellyn*
William Geoffrey Lowndes
    Frith Lowndes
*Malcolm Marshall*
*Roy Marshall*
Rajesh Maru
Dimitri Mascarenhas
Neil McCorkell
H.C. McDonell
*C. Phil Mead*
Tony Middleton
Richard Henry Moore
Alan Mullally
*John Alfred Newman*

*Mark Nicholas*
David O'Sullivan
Bobby Parks
Nick Pocock
Major R.M. Poore
A.E. 'Sam' Pothecary
John Rice
*Barry Richards*
Andy Roberts
Charles Robson
Neville Rogers
*Peter Sainsbury*
*Derek Shackleton*
*Chris Smith*
*Robin Smith*
Tom Soar
*Edward Mark Sprot*
Bob Stephenson
Jimmy Stone
Mike Taylor
*Lionel Tennyson*
Paul Terry
Bryan S.V. Timms
Tim Tremlett
David Turner
Shaun Udal
Richard Peter Hugh Utley
Clifford Walker
Donald Frederick Walker
Shane Warne
Alan Wassell
David White
*Edward George Wynyard*

The twenty who appear here in *italics*, occupy two pages instead of the usual one.

# Cecil Halliday Abercrombie
RHB, 1913

**Born:** 12 April 1886, Mozufferpore, India
**Died:** 31 May 1916, Jutland

Batting

| M | I | NO | Runs | Av |
|----|----|------|------|-------|
| 13 | 25 | 1 | 920 | 38.33 |

| 50 | 100 | ct/st |
|----|-----|-------|
| 2 | 3 | 6 |

Bowling

| O | M | Runs | Wkts | Av |
|----|---|------|------|--------|
| 45 | 4 | 166 | 1 | 166.00 |

| 5wI | 10wM |
|-----|------|
| - | - |

**Best Performances**
165 v. Essex, Leyton, 1913

Lt Cecil Abercrombie had a brief and exceptional career in cricket. Of a number of regular members of the armed forces who stepped into the Hampshire side between 1895 and 1925, and more than held their own, he stands foremost, for the fine season he enjoyed in 1913. This was his first and last for the county. He had already attracted some attention in 1911 when he hit 99 at Lord's for the Navy against the Army, and rather more the next summer when he reached three figures against the same opponents. A big, fast forward, he played rugby six times for Scotland.

His premier appearance in first-class cricket was spectacular: against Oxford University at Southampton he played innings of 126 and 39. In the first innings he batted without taking a chance and with Alex Bowell (193) added 142 runs in 75 minutes, reaching his own hundred at the same time, with the aid of 17 fours. Three matches later, he hit the headlines again at Dudley with a score of 144 which occupied only two and a quarter hours, while 233 runs were added and included a huge clean drive over the press box for six, a five and 17 fours. His play was faultless until, as one reporter put it, he became reckless.

It was in the next match that he reached his highest point when, in partnership with George Brown, he saved the day against Essex at Leyton in spectacular fashion. Hampshire were dismissed cheaply in the first innings in response to the Essex total of 507 and followed on 376 behind. They had been reduced to 198 for 6 in spite of a fine century by Tennyson. Abercrombie and Brown played themselves in steadily, but gradually mastered the Essex attack and in a great display of hitting added 325 runs in three and a half hours, which remains a county record for the seventh wicket. Brown's score was an undefeated 140, and Abercrombie had reached 165 when he was splendidly caught in the long field. His strokes included 4 sixes, a five and 11 fours. The pair also stole many quick singles, and converted ones into twos. After missing two matches, he never quite hit the same form again, although he hit 79 against Somerset at Portsmouth (occupying only 100 minutes, and the only total over 30 in the innings) and 65 in the game with Gloucestershire at Bournemouth, when he was last out after hitting 11 fours.

When his season ended with a rain-spoiled match at Leicester, he had played 13 matches for 25 innings and scored 920 runs at an average of 38.33. He received a letter of congratulations from the county secretary, F.H. Bacon, who looked forward to an encouraging future with Hampshire for him. It never happened. His naval service prevented him playing at all in 1914 and two years later he was lost when his ship, HMS *Defence*, was sunk at the Battle of Jutland. Bacon had already perished at sea in the previous October.

**Born:** 4 May 1902, London
**Died:** 16 August 1986, Yapton

### Batting

| M | I | NO | Runs | Av |
|---|---|----|------|-----|
| 108 | 175 | 13 | 3603 | 22.24 |
| 50 | 100 | ct/st | | |
| 10 | 4 | 41 | | |

### Bowling

| O | M | Runs | Wkts | Av |
|---|---|------|------|-----|
| 40.2 | 2 | 191 | 2 | 95.50 |
| 5wI | 10wM | | | |
| - | - | | | |

### Best Performances
159 v. Leicestershire, Leicester, 1928

Ronnie Aird devoted his life, except for one notable gap, to cricket. As an elegant stroke player, he was in the eleven at Eton for three years, scoring a match-winning century in 1921 against Winchester, for whom John Guise had just contributed 278. At first-class level his progress was slow: he did not get his blue at Cambridge until 1923, and only fulfilled expectations for Hampshire the following year when he played regularly and hit two fine hundreds and scored 1,072 runs at an average of 24.36. Against Sussex at Hastings, he and Phil Mead shared in a partnership which added 266 in four hours. That was his only full season and he subsequently became one of those players who often performed well on rare appearances and with little practice, for example in his innings of 159 out of 272 against Leicestershire in 1928, when he played only twice for the county.

Meanwhile, in 1926, he was appointed assistant secretary to MCC and worked under two secretaries, W. Findlay and R.S. Rait Kerr, until he succeeded as secretary in 1952. In the post he was completely imperturbable, always suave and courteous. MCC was not in a mood for change during his time, but Aird was a popular and competent figure. He retired in 1962, but was president of MCC in 1968/69 and a trustee from 1971 to 1983. As president, he chaired a highly contentious special meeting on relations with South Africa, of which his handling was greatly admired. He was also president of Hampshire from 1971 to 1986, sixty-six years after his first appearance for the county.

In the Second World War, he served in the 10th Armoured Division in which, in the words of his citation for an immediate MC, he showed the greatest gallantry and devotion to duty in many tank battles. On 31 August 1942 in North Africa, his squadron was attacked by over sixty tanks. Undaunted by the severe penetration of his tank and the death of the driver, he reorganised his crew under fire, kept the battle line unbroken and succeeded in knocking out at least two German tanks. It is small wonder then, that after an experience like that little disturbed him at Lord's.

# Harry Surtees Altham
RHB, 1919-1923

**Born:** 30 November 1888, Camberley
**Died:** 11 March 1965, Sheffield

Batting

| M | I | NO | Runs | Av |
|----|-----|------|------|-------|
| 24 | 38 | 6 | 713 | 22.28 |
| 50 | 100 | ct/st | | |
| 2 | 1 | 15 | | |

Bowling

| O | M | Runs | Wkts | Av |
|----|-----|------|------|-----|
| 3 | 0 | 11 | 0 | - |
| 5wI | 10wM | | | |
| - | - | | | |

**Best Performances**
141 v. Kent, Canterbury, 1921

Harry Altham cut a more than useful figure at school and county level, aggregating more runs (606, average 46.84) in 1908 than any other member of the Repton XI, seven of whom went on to play county cricket. Altham first played for Surrey in that same year. He was an Oxford blue in 1911 and 1912. It was good fortune for Hampshire when he became a master at Winchester College in the following year. First, as a player until 1923, and later as an administrator, he rendered over forty-five years' service to Hampshire. His one big innings came in the hour of need, 141 in only three hours and fifteen minutes against Kent at Canterbury in 1921. In a long career in club cricket he was formidable, achieving his highest score of 236 not out for the Harlequins against Mote Park in 1920.

He served on the Hampshire Committee for over 40 years and was a most active president from 1947 until his death in 1965. At the same time, he pursued a succession of important roles for MCC: he joined the Committee in 1941, and was treasurer from 1950 until 1963. He chaired the MCC Cricket Enquiry Committee which looked into the welfare of English cricket in 1949, helped to found the MCC Youth Cricket Association and became its first chairman and was also the first president of the English Schools Cricket Association. He was an enthusiastic propagandist for modern coaching methods and a skilful coach himself.

Altham was Chairman of Selectors of the successful MCC side for Australia in 1954/55, yet, in spite of this vast contribution to the development of cricket in his time, in the long term, Altham is best remembered as cricket's historian. He was the author of *A History of Cricket* (which first appeared in serial form in *The Cricketer* magazine in 1922) followed by four subsequent editions, in which he collaborated with E.W. Swanton. He was a joint author of *Hampshire County Cricket – The Official History 1957* and wrote many articles published in *Wisden*, the *Hampshire Handbook*, and elsewhere; and always, in speeches and in writing, he extolled the eighteenth-century cricketers of the Hambledon Club with diligence and affection. Those qualities were apparent in his dealings as a schoolmaster, housemaster and coach. No one could have been more patient when I, as a fourteen year old, standing on a chair, tried (and failed any number of times) to drop a ball in a marked circle for him to essay the cover drive.

Hampshire's historians have an exceptionally hard act to follow. Harry Altham's material was scrupulously researched and elegantly written, as the product of an education which formed an enquiring cast of mind, reinforced by profound learning. His *History of Cricket*, first produced in 1926, has stood the test of time.

**Born:** 25 February 1914, Basingstoke
**Died:** 14 December 1991, Alderney

craggy, tough perhaps, but something near to being a master craftsman of defensive batting.' Of Mike Brearley, a close friend, he commented, 'He is not a great batsman, but he is an extremely good one, partly because he assesses both his capabilities and his purpose clearly ... he is ... basically orthodox but, again, a pragmatist. For all his native ability, he is not an instinctive player as many of the great batsmen have been. Characteristically, he tries to evaluate every ball in its context.' His description of Barry Richards reads, 'Once in two or three generations there comes a batsman who beguiles even his opponents; such is Barry Richards; no one recognises superlative cricket more clearly than an English professional cricketer. When he plays a major innings, it appeals to both the savage and the artist in us. He butchers bowling, hitting with a savage power, the more impressive for being vested by the certainty of his timing.'

John Arlott was a voracious writer, never happier than when combining insight with a meticulous selection of words. The magnetic effect of John's writing on the reader disguises the trouble he took to convey exactly the impression he wanted to make, whether writing or speaking, and whether in public or as host at his own table; he was a conjuror of ideas. He could be affronted by anything slipshod but, as by nature the most kind and gentle of men, he always tried to conceal the affront – unless the subject were apartheid in South Africa, which he had seen at first hand, and abominated.

He had long been the most familiar voice on radio when he retired from cricket commentary in 1980. He moved from Alresford to Alderney, where he felt the cleaner air and proximity of the continent were advantageous. His access to his friends wasn't as good, which was a disadvantage to such a gregarious man, but a stream of visitors made the forty-minute flight to enjoy the almost boundless hospitality provided by Pat and himself, and even the decline in his health did not reduce their volume.

Compared to Altham, John Arlott approached cricket from a different viewpoint, that of a poet. It was poetry which first introduced him to the listening public before he was thirty, and which formed the material for his first books. His training as a policeman encouraged his eye for detail, and his affection for his fellow man as well as for cricket made him a formidable observer and chronicler. If it is asked why he, for all his merits, should be included in a book about Hampshire cricketers, the answer is that it would not be complete without him.

John Arlott did appear on the field for the County one day at Worcester in 1938, as twelfth man in borrowed gear, and in the 1960s, he was an elected member of the County Club Committee. Above all, he wrote about the cricketers of his time with both affection for their characters and critical discernments of their ability. The affection was returned and for many years until his death he was the elected president of the Players Union. His analyses of technique were masterly. Of Neville Rogers, he wrote '... he became the typical "modern" batsman. His judgement of the swinging ball, his ability to pull his bat away in face of late movement in the air, were masterly in their lack of hurry. He would calmly take on his pads or thigh the ball, missing his leg stump by a bare two or three inches, or refrain from "slip-bait" fractionally outside the off ... as a cricketer,

# John Arnold
RHB, RM, 1929-1950

**Born:** 30 November 1907, Cowley, Oxford
**Died:** 3 April 1984, Southampton

**Batting**

| M | I | NO | Runs | Av |
|---|---|----|------|-----|
| 396 | 701 | 45 | 21596 | 35.92 |

| 50 | 100 | ct/st | | |
|----|-----|-------|---|---|
| 116 | 36 | 181 | | |

**Bowling**

| O | M | Runs | Wkts | Av |
|---|---|------|------|-----|
| 248.1 | 20 | 1182 | 17 | 69.52 |

| 5wI | 10wM |
|-----|------|
| - | - |

**Best Performances**
227 *v.* Glamorgan, Cardiff, 1932
3/34 *v.* Kent, Southampton, 1930

Johnnie Arnold was one of a line of good batsmen, and men of character, from Oxfordshire, who rendered great service to Hampshire over a period of fifty years. Alec Bowell, George Brown, Lofty Herman, Neville Rogers and Alan Castell were the others. He played first for Hampshire in one match in 1929, when enjoying a splendid season for his native county and, qualifying at the end of May 1930, had the pleasure of completing 1,000 runs in his first season of first-class county cricket. He could never have anticipated that within a year he would be opening the batting for England at Lord's.

In 1931, with England's established openers no longer available, Jack Hobbs retired and Herbert Sutcliffe handicapped by a strain, the selectors chose Arnold and the young Northamptonshire batsman, Bakewell, to lead off for England. Arnold's scores were nought and 34 and he never gained selection again. A subsequent appearance for England at Association Football (he was a quick moving centre half for Southampton and Fulham) gave him the rare status of a double international. In the summer of 1934, he hit seven centuries, including 109 not out for Hampshire *v.* the Australians and 125 for Players *v.* the Gentlemen at the Oval. His season's aggregate reached 2,261 at an average of 48.10. He then settled into the role of a good County player (although, as if to show the selectors a thing or two, he developed a penchant for hitting hundreds against touring sides – the Indians (1932), the Australians (1934), the South Africans (1947) and the New Zealanders (1949)), scoring his sixteen or seventeen hundred runs a year, and once Phil Mead had withdrawn, usually heading the County averages.

This was as true in 1946 as it had been in 1937 and 1939. His second most successful season came in 1947 when his five centuries included 195 *v.* Gloucestershire at Bournemouth, and 188 *v.* Northamptonshire at Southampton, and his total number of runs was 1,783, average 41.16. In July 1950, he was at the top of the batting table again, with scores of 141 against Essex and 107 at Trent Bridge to his credit. He had reached fifty in each innings against Yorkshire at Bradford but was well below form at Derby. After this, he played no more, as he had been overtaken by serious illness. It was several years before the large gap he left was filled by the qualification of Roy Marshall in 1955.

Johnnie Arnold used a wide range of strokes; he was especially strong in pulling and driving. He excelled at cover point, tearing across the ground and returning the ball with a low, quick and accurate throw. A man of great charm, he was as popular off the field as he was on it. He was a first-class umpire from 1961 to 1974.

# Jon Ayling
RHB, RFM, 1988-1993

**Born:** 13 June 1967, Portsmouth

**Batting**

| M | I | NO | Runs | Av |
|---|---|----|------|-----|
| 60 | 90 | 12 | 2082 | 26.69 |
| 50 | 100 | ct/st | | |
| 11 | 1 | 17 | | |

**Bowling**

| O | M | Runs | Wkts | Av |
|---|---|------|------|-----|
| 1229 | 281 | 3405 | 134 | 25.41 |
| 5wI | 10wM | | | |
| 1 | - | | | |

**Best Performances**
121 v. Oxford University, Oxford, 1992
5/12 v. Middlesex, Bournemouth, 1992

There are few things sadder in sport than to see a highly promising career cut short by injury. Such was the fate of the Portsmouth-born all-rounder Jon Ayling, who appeared in a Lord's final and was being talked of as a potential England player within weeks of his first-class debut. Only nine months later, he was to suffer an injury so grave that it was to force his retirement from professional cricket at the age of twenty-five.

Ayling played a few one-day games at the end of the 1987 season, but he soon made himself invaluable in both forms of the game. In three-day cricket in 1988, he made 711 runs at 24.51 in nineteen games as well as taking 47 wickets at 23.56 with his fast-medium bowling. Oddly enough, it took him longer to get established in the one-day side and he missed all the preliminary rounds of the Benson & Hedges Cup. He did not take long to make an impact once he got in the side, dismissing Graeme Hick with his third ball in the competition as Hampshire beat Worcestershire in the quarter-final. In the final, he bowled nine overs for 21 runs and took a wicket.

It was in the following spring that disaster struck. In a pre-season friendly v. Sussex, Ayling, tall and wiry but slender, collided with the heavyweight Sussex batsman David Smith. The resulting knee injury meant that he would have to miss the whole of that season. Even so, the critical long-term implications of the injury were still not fully apparent.

The temptation to recall such a thorough-bred all-rounder as soon as possible was hard to resist in 1990, and there were times when playing seemed a bit of a struggle for Ayling. He was Hampshire's leading wicket-taker in the Sunday League but he played only nine first-class matches and took 11 wickets.

In 1991, he played little more first-class cricket but this time he topped the County's bowling averages. There were some batting highlights too. Against Middlesex at Lord's, he supported David Gower in a thrilling run chase and won the match with a six off the fourth ball of the last over. There was an echo of this in the NatWest final against Surrey when he was also at the crease in the gloom for the last tense overs in which he again hit the winning runs in the last over. This was an old head on young shoulders.

In 1992, Ayling again topped the bowling averages with 48 wickets at 20.60 in eighteen games. He played in the Benson & Hedges final against Kent – one of four men to have played in each of Hampshire's three finals. Promise seemed to be on the verge of fulfil-ment when the medical prognosis on his dam-aged knee compelled retirement before the start of the 1993 season.

# Adrian Aymes

RHB, WKT, 1987-2002

**Born:** 4 June 1964, Southampton

**Batting**

| M | I | NO | Runs | Av |
|---|---|---|---|---|
| 215 | 314 | 79 | 7338 | 31.22 |
| **50** | **100** | **ct/st** | | |
| 38 | 8 | 516/44 | | |

**Bowling**

| O | M | Runs | Wkts | Av |
|---|---|---|---|---|
| 41 | 0 | 438 | 6 | 73.00 |
| **5wI** | **10wM** | | | |
| - | - | | | |

**Best Performances**
133 v. Leicestershire, Leicester, 1998
2/101 v. Nottinghamshire, Nottingham, 2001

Adi Aymes came to Hampshire straight from club cricket with Hursley Park, near Winchester, and for over a decade has been one of the most accomplished wicketkeeper-batsmen in the country. He made his debut in 1987 against Surrey at the Oval scoring 58 in his only innings. Bobby Parks was still very much the man in possession and Aymes had to be content with second-eleven cricket, although he equalled Parks's record of ten dismissals in a match against Oxford University in 1989. In 1990, he played in the last five games of the season and in eight innings, four of them not out, scored 317 runs at an average of 79.

He started 1991 as first-choice wicketkeeper and has remained so ever since. Until 2002, he had only two significant spells out through injury, a tribute to his consistently high level of fitness. The first was in 1992 when he damaged a knee and had to miss the Benson & Hedges Cup final. The second came at the start of his benefit season, which was 2000, and coincided with the arrival at Hampshire of Shane Warne. Manfully, Derek Kenway coped behind the stumps, but Aymes' absence in those early weeks played a part in Hampshire's woefully disappointing season.

Even the best wicketkeepers fall into two categories: those who make an impact because of their volubility or quirkiness, and those who conduct operations on a more self-effacing basis. Aymes is one of the former and his chivvying presence clearly makes an impact on those around him. Tall for a 'keeper at 6ft, he is nonetheless extremely agile, very competent and dependable and good standing up to the stumps, which is always the acid test. Indeed, he is happy to stand up to someone with the pace of Dimitri Mascarenhas and has made stumpings off him.

While never managing to average more than 79 in a season, his batting has still been extremely valuable, particularly as Hampshire's top order has often had a fragile look in recent years. He scored his maiden century in 1993 against Sussex (in a game which achieved the highest aggregate of runs in a Hampshire Championship match) and has scored eight centuries in all. Two of them came in successive matches in 1998, when Robin Smith took the decision to promote Aymes to number 5 in the order. His 133 not out against Leicestershire is the eighth-highest score by a Hampshire wicketkeeper, and he must have come close to being selected to tour Australia that winter. In 2001, he showed no diminution of his powers either with the bat or behind the stumps and, despite the signing of Nic Pothas, only injury prevented him from starting 2002 as first-choice wicketkeeper for Championship matches.

**Born:** 24 June 1869, Colombo, Ceylon
**Died:** 31 October 1915, off Belgian coast

**Batting**

| M | I | NO | Runs | Av |
|---|---|----|------|-----|
| 75 | 132 | 11 | 1909 | 15.77 |
| 50 | 100 | ct/st | | |
| 5 | 1 | 34 | | |

**Bowling**

| O | M | Runs | Wkts | Av |
|---|---|------|------|-----|
| 36.1 | 3 | 190 | 6 | 31.66 |
| 5wI | 10wM | | | |
| - | - | | | |

**Best Performances**
110 v. Leicestershire, Southampton, 1907
2/23 v. Lancashire, Manchester, 1911

In 1903, F.H. Bacon became the first paid secretary to Hampshire County Cricket Club when the vast increase in administration made it impossible for the honorary secretary, Russell Bencraft, to continue. Under Bacon's genial, but watchful eye, membership increased, the playing staff was extended, and the fixture list increased, while the seasons of 1908 to 1914 proved to be ones of hitherto unparalleled success on the field. He was responsible for the introduction as professionals of Jack Newman and Walter Livsey into the Hampshire team. Earlier, he had played for the County as a professional, and in his very first match, v. Warwickshire at Edgbaston in 1894, he scored a faultless 114 in 130 minutes. It was unfortunate for him that Hampshire's fixtures did not enjoy first-class status until the following year. He continued playing when the need arose after he became secretary, and hit a second hundred, 110, against Leicestershire in 1907. Small in stature (he stood 5ft 5in), he was a free hitter, and for some years was among the best cover points in England. Playing as an amateur after his appointment as secretary, he was one of the few cricketers of his time who played first as a professional and afterwards as an amateur. He was in the eleven at St Augustine's College, Canterbury, and subsequently played for Basingstoke, for whom three not out innings, each of 101, led to his trial for Hampshire.

This small, genial, enthusiastic man was an early volunteer for the Royal Naval Reserve in the First World War, although at the age of forty-five, he could have stayed at home. He was drowned off the Belgian coast when the patrol ship on which he was serving as assistant paymaster was mined, in October 1915.

# John Badcock
### RFM, RHB, 1906-1908

**Born:** 4 October 1883, Christchurch, Hants
**Died:** 24 August 1940, Marylebone, London

### Batting

| M | I | NO | Runs | Av |
|---|---|---|---|---|
| 63 | 102 | 19 | 1199 | 14.44 |
| **50** | **100** | **ct/st** | | |
| 2 | - | 30 | | |

### Bowling

| O | M | Runs | Wkts | Av |
|---|---|---|---|---|
| 1526.1 | 245 | 5414 | 212 | 25.53 |
| **5wI** | **10wM** | | | |
| 12 | 3 | | | |

### Best Performances
74 *v.* Middlesex, Southampton, 1907
8/44 *v.* Sussex, Portsmouth, 1908

Surely, no player has had a greater impact on Hampshire cricket in his first season than John Badcock from Kent in 1906, not Roy Marshall, nor Matthew Hayden, nor even Shane Warne. He was Hampshire-born, at Christchurch, but was taken on by the Tonbridge nursery. As he had no hope of displacing Arthur Fielder, the Kent fast bowler, he returned home to fortify his native county, which certainly needed bolstering, as their record over the previous six seasons showed only 13 wins compared to 69 defeats.

The results showed a gradual build-up of confidence as the season progressed, and after the side beat the West Indians at the beginning of July, they won six County matches, while losing only one. For Badcock himself, returns of six for 85 against the strong Surrey batting, when his victims included both Tom Hayward and Jack Hobbs, six for 63 *v.* Derbyshire, and six Northamptonshire batsmen for 61 were joined by nine in the match with Worcestershire, and eight each *v.* Leicestershire and in the other game with Derby. Nothing would have given him greater satisfaction than his performance in June against his former colleagues at Tonbridge, six

of them falling to his fast bowling at the cost of 81 runs, as well as his making top score in Hampshire's first innings.

John Badcock was a tall, well-built player at his best, but even during that debut season, when he finished with 96 wickets at an average of 24.81, there were comments about his bulk. In 1907, a damp season less suited to a bowler of his pace, his victims fell to 46, and he developed a tendency to bowl no-balls – as many as 46 in Championship matches, although he did score 559 runs. He fared better in 1908, capturing 67 wickets in the Championship, average 26.17, including the best performance of his career, eight wickets for 28 against Sussex at Portsmouth. By now, the county committee were looking for a trainer to get Badcock into prime condition, at which he may have taken offence, as at the end of the following winter, after several reminders, he declined the contract offered to him the previous October, and played no more. He died of peritonitis early in the Second World War, when he was working as manager of a cinema. The rumour that C.L. Badcock, the Tasmanian who toured England with Bradman's touring side in 1938, was his son, is untrue.

LHB, SLA, 1927-1952

**Born:** 6 April 1908, Shawford
**Died:** 9 February 1988, Southampton

**Batting**

| M | I | NO | Runs | Av |
|---|---|---|---|---|
| 242 | 408 | 35 | 9302 | 24.93 |
| 50 | 100 | ct/st | | |
| 51 | 5 | 62 | | |

**Bowling**

| O | M | Runs | Wkts | Av |
|---|---|---|---|---|
| 5038 | 1291 | 12595 | 467 | 26.97 |
| 5wl | 10wM | | | |
| 25 | 5 | | | |

**Best Performances**
133 v. Worcestershire, Southampton, 1946
7/7 v. Nottinghamshire, Southampton, 1932

Jim Bailey made his Hampshire debut in 1927. Photographs of the period show a slim, elegant young man, often wearing a blazer and cravat.

Bailey became an outstanding county cricketer, although the journey, ending in his retirement from professional cricket in 1949, had been complex, often frustrating and as interesting as the man himself was.

After his debut, he took two or three years to break into the side. In 1930, young Johnny Arnold established himself as George Brown's opening partner and, at the start of the following season, Jim Bailey replaced the veteran Brown. Arnold and Bailey shared century partnerships together in their first two matches in May, but this form was not maintained. Although Jim's form was somewhat disappointing (a season's average of just 20), he scored his maiden century in the last innings of the season v. Nottinghamshire.

In 1932, he began as an opening batsman, but having made just 107 runs in eight innings, he dropped down the order. More impressively, he took 69 wickets at 22 each and began to look more like an all-rounder.

The Oxfordshire opening partnership of Brown and Arnold continued in 1933 when Jim made 923 runs. Sadly, it was the turn of his bowling to fall away completely and he took just eight wickets. At the end of that season, he moved to Middlesex to qualify by residence. After two frustrating seasons, he accepted an invitation to play as a professional for Accrington – a previous home for Hampshire's C.B. Llewellyn – in the Lancashire League. He took a wicket with his first ball and generally sustained this excellent start with runs and wickets. Accrington won the Worsley Cup for the first time. The following year he set a club record of 6 consecutive fifties, achieved a record aggregate for Accrington and became the first Accrington batsman and the first English professional to score 1,000 runs in a season.

In 1938, Hampshire persuaded him to appear in northern mid-week fixtures. In September, Hampshire offered him a full-time contract and Jim came back to his native county.

In 1939, he scored 1,329 runs and scored his first County century since 1933. He also took a few wickets during the season, including 6-72 against Leicestershire in late July.

After the war, although approaching middle age, he returned to County cricket with relish. In 1948, at the age of forty, Jim Bailey finally fulfilled all that youthful promise and became the fourth and last Hampshire player to do the first-class double of 1,000 runs and 100 wickets, topping both averages for his county. *Wisden* recorded that his season was 'a triumph', adding that Jim 'batted with remarkable consistency and his final figures show him as the most successful left-arm slow bowler in the country.'

He was almost as successful in 1949 with 1,254 runs and 86 wickets. Jim then retired, although in 1952 he returned for a single match, the season's first at Edgbaston. In his retirement, he spent many happy days at Northlands Road and was at one time on the committee.

# Harry Baldwin
RHB, ROB, 1877-1905

**Born:** 27 November 1860, Wokingham
**Died:** 12 January 1935, Aldershot

**Batting**

| M | I | NO | Runs | Av |
|---|---|----|------|-----|
| 150 | 240 | 65 | 1863 | 10.64 |
| **50** | **100** | **ct/st** | | |
| 1 | - | 54 | | |

**Bowling**

| O | M | Runs | Wkts | Av |
|---|---|------|------|-----|
| 5674.1 | 2108 | 14336 | 580 | 24.71 |
| **5wI** | **10wM** | | | |
| 41 | 6 | | | |

**Best Performances**
55* v. Worcestershire at Worcester, 1905
8/74 v. Sussex, Hove, 1898

In many Hampshire team photographs of the late Victorian and Edwardian eras, Harry Baldwin stands in the back row, heavily built and heavily moustached under his county cap. He first played for the County in 1877, but his greatest days came when they regained first-class status in 1895 – his total of 114 wickets that season remained a County record until 1902 and, in Championship matches, he and Tom Soar captured 191 victims between them compared to the other fourteen bowlers' 69. In the first Championship game at Southampton, he and Soar bowled unchanged to gain Hampshire an innings victory over Derbyshire, while against Essex at Southampton, 13 of the opposition fell to him at the cost of 76 runs. Baldwin also had 8 victims when the county beat Yorkshire inside two days at Sheffield in August. Not until the match against Warwickshire, which began on 19 August, did Baldwin fail to capture at least one wicket in an innings. These were heady days, but in subsequent years he had to work much harder for his wickets – 1899 brought him 78 victims, average 27, while the next year his 84 victims – at a slightly increased average – were more than double those of any other bowler. Of 22 matches, Hampshire lost 16 and drew the remainder.

He rather fancied his chances as a batsman. He had at least one century to his credit – 113 not out in a minor counties match in 1890. In his last season, 1905, he hit his highest first-class score, 55 not out against Worcestershire at Worcester.

Baldwin dropped out of the side in 1901, but returned in 1904 and 1905, when the attack was still desperately weak. In this last season, he still took twice as many wickets as any other member of the attack. Bad luck haunted Harry Baldwin, who lost nine seasons in his prime when Hampshire forfeited first-class status between 1886 and 1894, and found his twenty-one years' service rewarded with a benefit match which was all over in one day. After his retirement, his services as a coach were in great demand, but in 1913 he was unemployed and had to ask the Hampshire Committee for financial help, which they readily offered. His son, also Harry, played for Surrey in the 1920s, and later became an umpire who achieved Test match status.

# Mike Barnard ———————————————————————
RHB, RFM, 1952-1966

**Born:** 18 July 1933, Portsmouth

**Batting**

| M | I | NO | Runs | Av |
|---|---|----|------|-----|
| 276 | 463 | 41 | 9314 | 22.07 |
| **50** | **100** | **ct/st** | | |
| 6 | 46 | 313 | | |

**Bowling**

| O | M | Runs | Wkts | Av |
|---|---|------|------|-----|
| 185.3 | 35 | 563 | 16 | 35.18 |
| **5wI** | **10wM** | | | |
| - | - | | | |

**Best Performances**
128* v. MCC, Lord's, 1956
128 v. Indians, Bournemouth, 1959
3/35 v. Oxford University, Oxford, 1954

Mike Barnard was a natural athlete, who shone sporadically as a forcing, right-handed batsman, but whose forte was his brilliance at first slip – in 276 appearances for Hampshire he held 313 catches. Pompey born and bred, Barnard was educated at the grammar school and played with distinction as an inside left for the football club, appearing in 116 First Division games and 7 FA Cup ties and scoring 24 goals between 1951 and 1959.

Barnard, one of a handful of Jewish first-class cricketers, was a 'Holt's Colt', making his debut in 1952. In the Championship campaign of 1955 when Hampshire came third, Barnard played in 25 games, scoring 908 runs, including his maiden Championship century (he scored a hundred against the Pakistan tourists in 1954) and holding 32 catches. He was capped and appeared to have established himself. However, he never provided quite the weight of runs needed to cement a regular place. A gap appeared in the middle order after the departure of Alan Rayment, but Barnard failed to secure the position.

Barnard, Denis Baldry and Danny Livingstone competed for two middle-order places in 1960 and 1961 with Barnard missing out initially but, as the Championship race reached its critical phase in the latter year, he forced his way into the team at Baldry's expense. In his second game back in the side, he scored 114 not out against Warwickshire, helping to set up a crucial win. He retained his place for the rest of the season and played a valuable role in the victory over Derbyshire which clinched the title for Hampshire, adding 99 in 68 minutes for the fifth wicket with Peter Sainsbury, as Hampshire pressed for a third-innings declaration.

He scored 1,000 runs in 1962 and over 900 in 1963 and 1965, opening the innings with Roy Marshall in the latter year. In 1964, he had made a splendid century against the Australians, opening in place of Marshall in a game which the County made a brave attempt to win. Mike Barnard's record in the Gillette Cup, in which Hampshire had limited success in the early days, suggested that his instinctively aggressive style was well-suited to the one-day game.

Soon after leaving the first-class game in 1966, Mike Barnard suffered the terrible misfortune of a serious leg injury in a car accident in Germany.

He has remained a familiar and friendly figure on Hampshire grounds through his work for local radio; he also organises the annual player reunions.

# Victor Alexander Barton

RHB, OB, 1895-1902

**Born:** 6 October 1867, Netley, Hants
**Died:** 23 March 1906, Southampton

### Batting

| M | I | NO | Runs | Av |
|---|---|----|------|-----|
| 143 | 261 | 13 | 6204 | 25.01 |

| 50 | 100 | ct/st | | |
|----|-----|-------|---|---|
| 30 | 6 | 95 | | |

### Bowling

| O | M | Runs | Wkts | Av |
|---|---|------|------|-----|
| 1589.1 | 556 | 3820 | 130 | 29.38 |

| 5wI | 10wM | | | |
|-----|------|---|---|---|
| 3 | - | | | |

### Best Performances

205 v. Sussex, Hove, 1900
6/28 v. Surrey, The Oval, 1901

Victor Barton was the most successful professional batsman to play for Hampshire before the arrival of Charles Llewellyn, Alec Bowell and Phil Mead early in the twentieth century. He was the first paid player to reach four figures in a season in 1899, and the first to a double century (203) in the same summer. Victor was a soldier, when he first came to public notice by making 91 and 102 for the Royal Horse Artillery at Mote Park, Maidstone, in 1889. This led to his selection for Kent in a few matches, and in 1890, after being bought out of the Army, he accompanied W.W. Read's touring team to South Africa. The tour ended with a three-day game at Cape Town v. Eleven of South Africa, subsequently recognised, not only as first-class, but given test match status. Barton contributed a score of 23 to an overwhelming victory by the tourists and he ranks as Hampshire's first international cricketer. Barton joined Hampshire in 1891, when he impressed by scoring 741 runs, average 39.

He made a major contribution in 1894 to the County's elevation to first-class status, scoring 689 runs at an average of 40.51, with a highest score of 95. He achieved a similar total in first-class cricket in 1895, but his average fell to 22, bouncing back again the following year when he reached 31.14 for his 789 runs. Wisden described his dashing display as the best thing in the county's cricket,

apart from the batting of E.G. Wynyard. In 1899, he scored 984 runs at 28 runs an innings, and with the help of his scores against the Australians, exceeded 1,000 runs.

In the dreadful season of 1900, when Hampshire lost 16 of their 22 matches (and drew the other six), Barton again achieved his 1,000 runs, and against Sussex at Brighton in July, he played the innings of his life. At the end of the second day when Hampshire faced a total of 407, he had scored 175 not out, and the next morning raised his total to 205. He batted brilliantly throughout this innings, making his runs in three hours and forty-five minutes. He had already bowled over 40 overs for 76 and three wickets in the Sussex first innings. In that season of 1900, when Tom Soar broke down, and the County tried numerous unsuccessful stand-ins, only Barton, with 38 wickets, average 36.15, gave any support to Harry Baldwin (of the 41 players who turned out in 1900, 28 had a turn with the ball). Barton bowled with more success in 1901, capturing 48 wickets at 22.20 each, in addition to his 876 runs. He was also a fine fielder at cover point.

When in 1902 he took a well-deserved benefit, he was already suffering from eye trouble, and retired from cricket at the end of the season. At one time, he ran a bat-making business; subsequently, he kept a pub, at Netley, on Southampton Water. His early death in 1906 was deeply mourned and a fund was set up for his wife and daughter. Russell Bencraft said of Barton, 'No more unassuming, gentlemanly cricketer ever trod the cricket field than Victor Barton.'

**Born:** 4 March 1858, Southampton
**Died:** 25 December 1943, Compton,
Winchester

**Batting**

| M | I | NO | Runs | Av |
|---|---|----|------|-----|
| 44 | 76 | 18 | 908 | 15.65 |
| **50** | **100** | **ct/st** | | |
| 2 | - | 32 | | |

**Bowling**

| O | M | Runs | Wkts | Av |
|---|---|------|------|-----|
| 59.1 | 23 | 185 | 5 | 37.00 |
| **5wI** | **10wM** | | | |
| - | - | | | |

**Best Performances**
62* *v.* Derbyshire, Southampton, 1895
2/15 *v.* Sussex, Portsmouth, 1882

Cold figures show that Russell Bencraft played 44 matches for Hampshire over twenty years from 1876 – that period includes a spell from 1886 to 1894 when the county was adjudged to lack first-class status, and many good scores of his, including 195 *v.* Warwickshire in 1889, do not count in the statistics. The figures themselves give no idea of his paramount role in Hampshire cricket. For a period of sixty years, he was the guiding spirit of the club, the honorary secretary when they regained first-class status in 1895 and their captain in that significant season. Over the next forty years, he held the offices of honorary secretary, giving up the work only when it had grown to demand the services of a full-time paid official, he was chairman for fifteen years and finally president.

Bencraft was born in the workhouse at Southampton, where his father was the medical officer, and educated at St Edward's School, Oxford, and St George's Hospital, London. He held a number of medical appointments in his native city, and over the years also became a leading business figure, and a director and then chairman of Southern Newspapers Ltd. He was a councillor and, for almost fifty years a magistrate, and was also closely involved with local charities. His sporting activity was not limited to cricket. When, following his receipt of a knighthood in 1924, a dinner was held in his honour – 420 sportsmen attended, representing no fewer than 20 different organisations to which he had made a contribution. In 1937 an even larger assembly attended a dinner to celebrate his sixty years' devotion to the county cricket club.

Sir Russell had first played for Hampshire in 1876, against Kent, led by Lord Harris, and when a meeting was held in 1879 to decide whether or not the club should be wound up, he was persuaded to become honorary secretary and, for two or three years, ran the club practically single-handed. He remembered seeing the Australian Aboriginals' team, which toured England in 1868, and he played against their white successors in 1880. He also served as president of Southampton St Mary's Football Club and was first president of the Southern Football League, as well as being active as a referee. In addition, he was president of the Hampshire Rugby Union. Nor should it be forgotten that while he was a medical student, he once scored six centuries in one week!

Sir Russell Bencraft – master of all he surveyed.

# Alec Bowell

RHB, RFM, 1902-1927

**Born:** 27 April 1880, Oxford
**Died:** 28 August 1957, Oxford

### Batting

| M | I | NO | Runs | Av |
|---|---|----|------|-----|
| 473 | 806 | 43 | 18466 | 24.20 |
| **50** | **100** | **ct/st** | | |
| 90 | 25 | 253/2 | | |

### Bowling

| O | M | Runs | Wkts | Av |
|---|---|------|------|-----|
| 496.3 | 78 | 1766 | 34 | 51.94 |
| **5wI** | **10wM** | | | |
| - | - | | | |

### Best Performances

204 v. Lancashire, Bournemouth, 1914
4/20 v. Warwickshire, Southampton, 1913

Alec Bowell was the first of a line of cricketers from Oxford to play professionally for Hampshire. As the pathfinder, Alec joined the exiguous groundstaff at Southampton when he was only nineteen. The County's playing situation was wretched in the period 1900 to 1905 (except for 1901 when J.G. Greig and H.V. Hesketh Prichard brought blessed, but fleeting relief), but Alec and his contemporary, Jimmy Stone, the wicketkeeper, improved their performances year by year. In 1905, he hit his first century and scored 883 runs, as an opening bat, and he went on to become an integral part of the side which fared so well between 1910 and 1923. He was most prolific in 1913, when his total runs, 1,627, included five centuries, the highest being 193 against Oxford University. He exceeded this in 1914 with his 204 against Lancashire at Bournemouth.

He was still good enough to reach four figures in 1926, when he and Phil Mead put on 248 for the fourth wicket against Worcestershire in only three hours and fifty minutes – a magnificent match-saving effort at a point when Hampshire had to get 508 to win or bat all day to achieve a draw. Against the same opponents in 1920, he and George Brown put on 204 for the first wicket, which remained a county record for 39 years.

1920 was a great season for Bowell and Brown. They began with stands of 185 against Leicestershire at Southampton and 183 against Yorkshire at Leeds. In 1921, he and Walter Livsey shared in a partnership of 192 for the last wicket, against Worcestershire, which does remain a county record to this day. In all, he hit 25 hundreds for Hampshire. He had an excellent pair of wrists, and was a fine cutter of the ball – he could drive with great power and certainty. He was capable of playing a fine innings on a rain-affected wicket, but he was, in proportion, a much more secure and consistent performer on hard wickets in hot summers, such as 1911 and 1913. He excelled in the field at cover point. His son, Norman, played once each for Hampshire and Northants – he died when the Japanese ship in which he was being conveyed as a prisoner of war was sunk by American fire. Norman left a legacy to Hampshire – it was he who persuaded his father to recommend Neville Rogers to the County.

# Stuart Boyes

RHB, SLA, 1920-1939

**Born:** 31 March 1899, Southampton
**Died:** 11 February 1973, Southampton

**Batting**

| M | I | NO | Runs | Av |
|---|---|----|------|----|
| 474 | 677 | 156 | 7515 | 14.42 |
| 50 | 100 | ct/st | | |
| 16 | 2 | 474 | | |

**Bowling**

| O | M | Runs | Wkts | Av |
|---|---|------|------|----|
| 13817 | 3798 | 33513 | 1415 | 23.68 |
| 5wI | 10wM | | | |
| 71 | 11 | | | |

**Best Performances**
104 *v.* Northamptonshire, Newport (IOW),
  1938
9/57 *v.* Somerset, Yeovil, 1938

Stuart Boyes stands in a unique position among Hampshire cricketers; he was the only professional to be awarded a county cap between 1914 and 1929. He is indeed the link between the 'old guard' of Phil Mead, Jack Newman, Alec Kennedy and George Brown, who provided the backbone of the Hampshire team for twenty-five years into the 1930s, and the younger generation of John Arnold, Neil McCorkell and Gerald Hill, who saw the team through to the 1950s.

If this suggests a slightly isolated figure, that may be accurate. From still being a junior professional in 1930, he rose to being the senior professional by 1937. He was tall, slim and graceful; a slow left-arm bowler who met with consistent success between 1922 and 1939, and sometimes touched greater heights. A useful right-hand bat, who did not hit a hundred until 1936 and followed this with another in 1938, the general view was that he might have fared better with greater encouragement. As a fielder at short leg, he was in the top class, quick in anticipation, agile and prehensile, setting a really high standard.

John Arlott's view was that his most considerable contribution to the game was as a fieldsman. He had a career record of 500 catches. Stuart Boyes performed the hat-trick twice, and in 1934 against Nottinghamshire at Trent Bridge returned bowling figures of 80 overs, 28 maidens, 138 runs and 3 wickets. The bowling performance which he remembered with greatest pleasure was against Somerset at Yeovil in 1938, when he captured 9 wickets in the first innings for 57 runs.

In 1939, he alone of the regular bowlers achieved a mastery of the eight-ball over, and he and Charles Knott were beginning to form a useful spin-bowling partnership when war brought Stuart Boyes' County career to an end. In fact, his cricket career was only half over. Between 1946 and 1963, he built up a new reputation among the young as cricket coach at Ampleford College in Yorkshire.

As a slow left-arm bowler, helped by his considerable height, he normally achieved flight, line and length, but was thought by some to be lacking in spin. According to John Arlott, when Lord Tennyson, roused by lack of action on the field, urged Boyes to spin the ball, he would reply, 'I'm spinning it as hard as I can, my lord', as bowling with his left hand, he snapped the fingers of his right 'but it won't turn on this.'

# George Brown

LHB, RFM, WKT, 1908-1933

**Born:** 6 October 1887, Cowley, Oxford
**Died:** 3 December 1964, Winchester

**Batting**

| M | I | NO | Runs | Av |
|---|---|----|------|-----|
| 539 | 900 | 46 | 22962 | 26.88 |
| 50 | 100 | ct/st | | |
| 96 | 37 | 484/51 | | |

**Bowling**

| O | M | Runs | Wkts | Av |
|---|---|------|------|-----|
| 5085.3 | 822 | 17857 | 602 | 29.66 |
| 5wI | 10wM | | | |
| 23 | 2 | | | |

**Best Performances**
232* v. Yorkshire, Leeds, 1920
8/55 v. Gloucestershire, Cheltenham, 1913

An early photograph shows George Brown as a member of a village team, perhaps at his birthplace, Cowley, Oxford. He must have been fifteen or so, but all his characteristics as an adult are there: the direct stare at the photographer, the upright stance, the firm grip on his bat, and the well-made physique.

At the age of twenty, he made his first appearance for Hampshire, perhaps through the influence of Alec Bowell, and from the following year established himself as a regular member of the side. His first Championship match was against Surrey at the Oval. He was not outfaced, scoring 19 and 27 not out, and followed up with a number of useful innings. By the end of the season, his aggregate was 530 runs, average 17.09, and with his medium to fast bowling, he took 39 wickets for 25.02 runs each. In 1911, he totalled 1,327 runs, average 27, and took 88 wickets at the cost of 25. After a lean time the next season, he scored 1,263 runs, average 25, in 1913, and his victims numbered 85. He was also a fine and often spectacular fielder, close in or on the leg side in the covers or mid-off, where no hit was too hard for him. He also found time to keep wicket when the regular stumper, Jimmy Stone, or his successor, Walter Livsey, was unavailable.

After the First World War, everything seemed to be going well for him when, following a successful time in the season of two-day matches in 1919, he struck a rich vein of run-scoring the following year. He hit 6 hundreds, including 232 not out against Yorkshire at Leeds, 230 v. Essex at Bournemouth, and 151 v. Warwickshire at Portsmouth. At Leeds, he added 183 for the first wicket with Bowell, and shared a partnership of 269 with Phil Mead for the third. He and E.I.M. Barrett added 280 together for the wicket against Warwickshire at Portsmouth, and in the match with Gloucestershire at Southampton, they exceeded that partnership by adding 321. He scored readily enough in 1921 to earn selection for the last three Tests; he kept wicket splendidly and opened his account by scoring 57 and 46 at Leeds. Australia's victory in that match gave them the series and they took matters rather easily in the remaining two Tests. Still, Brown contributed 31 to an opening stand of 65 for the first wicket in the draw at Manchester, and made 32 and 84 in another inconclusive match at the Oval.

These performances were the highlight of his career – his form over the next four seasons proved highly variable and often disappointing. He kept wicket in four more Tests for England in South Africa in 1922/23, but hardly made a run. He made three other tours abroad with MCC to the West Indies in 1909/10, which was too early in his career, and with Sir Julien Cahn's team to Jamaica in 1931/32, which, perversely, was rather late. The other trip was with MCC to India, in 1926/27, under the captaincy of Arthur

50 after two hours of batting, and added 85 with W.R. de la C. Shirley, putting Hampshire with seven wickets down, only 54 ahead. Then Brown, whose hundred had occupied 185 minutes, initially farmed the bowling to protect the number 10 batsman, Walter Livsey, from Howell, who had wreaked the damage in Hampshire's first innings. As Livsey grew in confidence and the Warwickshire bowling lost its terrors, the game swung right away from Warwickshire who, eventually set 314 to win, lost the moral advantage and were defeated by 155 runs. Brown's contribution had been 172 and in the next match, he scored 153 against Glamorgan – in his other 45 innings of 1922, he totalled only 586 runs, average 13.02!

George Brown was too exceptional a cricketer not to recover his form, and in 1926, with the aid of six centuries, he reached 2,000 runs in the season for the only time at the age of thirty-eight. That year he was selected again for England against Australia for the final Test at the Oval, but he was injured while keeping wicket for Hampshire, and was not fit to play. He hit four more centuries in 1927 when his total runs were 1,674. That year, with Phil Mead, he added 344 against Yorkshire at Portsmouth. After the retirement of Livsey, George Brown, at the age of forty-two, became Hampshire's regular wicketkeeper for two seasons before, somewhat to his relief, Neil McCorkell was introduced into the side. He continued scoring his 1,000 runs a season until 1933. Subsequently, he was a first-class umpire, to which he was temperamentally unsuited; he was coach at the Royal Military Academy, Sandhurst, and later kept a pub in Winchester.

Gilligan. There, Brown played well as a member of a fairly strong team.

In county cricket, he gave useful support with the ball to Kennedy, Newman and Boyes. His most celebrated innings of all came from one of his mediocre seasons. At Edgbaston in 1922, Warwickshire followed their score of 223 by putting their visitors out for 15. Brown's was one of eight ducks in this shambles. Following on 208 runs in arrears, Hampshire struggled to 177 for 6 on what was still only the second morning of this match. Brown, who had gone in at number 6, reached

This gifted cricketer was at the mercy of an unpredictable temperament; he could score freely, almost with abandon, but could also sink into his shell, without any regard to the quality of the bowling he had to face. A man who scored 2,000 runs and twice took over 80 wickets in a season, fielded finely wherever he was put, and kept wicket in tests against Australia, has his niche in the history of cricket.

# Mervyn Burden
RHB, ROB, 1953-1963

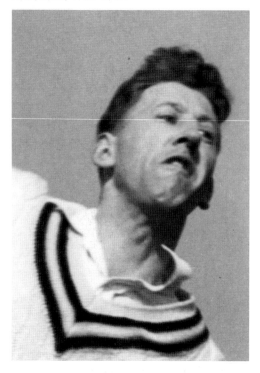

**Born:** 4 October 1930, Southampton
**Died:** 9 November 1987, Whitechurch

### Batting

| M | I | NO | Runs | Av |
|---|---|----|------|-----|
| 174 | 191 | 59 | 901 | 6.82 |

| 50 | 100 | ct/st | | |
|----|-----|-------|---|---|
| 1 | - | 76 | | |

### Bowling

| O | M | Runs | Wkts | Av |
|---|---|------|------|-----|
| 4868.1 | 1563 | 12559 | 481 | 26.11 |

| 5wI | 10wM | | | |
|-----|------|---|---|---|
| 23 | 4 | | | |

### Best Performances
51 *v.* Warwickshire, Portsmouth, 1960
8/38 *v.* Somerset, Frome, 1961

An off-spinner of the old school and a character to be relished, Mervyn Burden was a skilful bowler who played a significant part in Hampshire's Championship victory in 1961. In the right conditions, Burden was a match-winner.

Southampton-born and, like Jimmy Gray, educated at King Edward VI School in the city, Burden made his debut in 1953. It did not take him long to make an impression. In his second game, against Surrey at Bournemouth – often a happy hunting ground for Burden – he took 6 for 70. He made steady progress in 1954, and in 1955, when Hampshire came third in the Championship, he made a significant contribution, taking 70 wickets at an average of just over 21. In 1958, when the County came second, he also put in some useful performances. Bournemouth again featured prominently – in three games there he took 5 for 25 and 6 for 84, as Somerset narrowly avoided defeat by an innings, 6 for 47 in a win over Lancashire and 7 for 72 as Yorkshire were bowled out for 126 in a drawn game at the end of the season.

By 1961, the slow left-armer Alan Wassell tended to be preferred as Peter Sainbury's slow-bowling partner, and the off-spinner hardly played in the second half of the season. Still, he came second to Derek Shackleton in the bowling averages in that Championship-winning year, taking 45 wickets at 21.51 in twelve games. Against Somerset at Frome in early May, he took a career-best 8 for 38, including a spell of five wickets for one run in 31 balls in the home side's first innings of 102, and 4-70 in the second; Hampshire won a low-scoring game by 18 runs. In the return match at Bournemouth, he took 7 for 72 in the fourth innings as Hampshire won by 63 runs. He actually played more in 1962, taking 65 first-class wickets at 30.38, but dropped out the following year.

A career batting average of 6.82 suggests that, unless he was an outstanding fielder, Burden might have had difficulties in an era when multi-tasking is expected of cricketers as of everyone else. He was not an outstanding fielder. Having said that, John Arlott tells the story of a match in which Brian Crump, of Northamptonshire, who hardly ever hit a six, was twice quite brilliantly caught on the boundary by Mervyn Burden. 'It has never yet been decided,' wrote Arlott, 'who was more surprised, striker or catcher.'

Mervyn Burden died in 1987 and was the first of the 1961 Champions to pass away.

# Vic Cannings

RFM, RHB, 1950-1959

**Born:** 3 April 1919, Bighton

**Batting**

| M | I | NO | Runs | Av |
|---|---|----|------|-----|
| 230 | 294 | 103 | 1888 | 9.88 |
| 50 | 100 | ct/st | | |
| - | - | 89 | | |

**Bowling**

| O | M | Runs | Wkts | Av |
|---|---|------|------|-----|
| 7950.3 | 2423 | 18091 | 834 | 21.69 |
| 5wI | 10wM | | | |
| 39 | 4 | | | |

**Best Performances**
43* *v.* Sussex, Portsmouth, 1955
7/52 *v.* Oxford University, Oxford, 1950

Vic Cannings was born in the Hampshire village of Bighton, and in his teens he played club cricket for Farnham, but his route to his County side was convoluted.

During the war, he was a member of the Palestine police and played cricket regularly in the Middle East, once taking six wickets against an Australian Forces XI captained by Lindsay Hassett. In 1946, Hampshire gave him a trial but could not afford to engage him. Instead, he joined Warwickshire and made his debut for them in May 1947.

He played throughout that season, taking 61 wickets and scoring 500 runs, but in the following two seasons, he found it much harder to hold his place. Meanwhile, Hampshire's veteran pace bowlers, 'Lofty' Herman and George Heath, had both retired. 'Shack' had just broken into the side but Hampshire were looking for bowlers and Vic Cannings met their requirements.

He and 'Shack' opened the bowling together for the first time in May 1950 at Lord's. They took three wickets each in dismissing Middlesex for 103, Vic claiming Jack Robertson and the Compton brothers; indeed, Denis became Vic's 'rabbit'. He then took 7-52 *v.* Oxford University. He was quickly awarded his second county cap (Buckinghamshire later became a third) and was established in the side.

In 1951, the opening partners both took over 100 wickets. In the following year 'Shack' and Vic bowled unchanged in a victory over Kent at Southampton. In their first innings, Kent recovered from 18-9 to 32 all out and Vic held 3 gully catches.

The Hampshire side improved in the mid-1950s and, in 1955, finished in third place for the first time in their history. Vic had 94 wickets at 17.63 and, while Roy Marshall strengthened the batting significantly, it was the all-round strength of the bowling which made such a difference. Vic particularly enjoyed a final ball against Kent when he had Doug Wright lbw to win the match.

In 1958, Malcolm Heath replaced Vic as the regular partner to Shackleton, but Cannings took 6-54 to set up Hampshire's first victory, *v.* Worcestershire at Portsmouth, and he finished the season with 44 wickets at 22 each.

At the age of forty, 1959 was Vic Cannings' final season. With 'Butch' White also emerging, he was never a regular player, but he took eight Surrey wickets in August which effectively ended their hopes of an eighth successive title.

After retiring, he spent many happy years coaching the cricketers at Eton College. For Hampshire, he took 834 wickets in 230 matches at 21.68 each – all after the age of thirty.

# Cardigan Connor

RHB, RFM, 1984-1996

**Born:** 24 March 1961, The Kalky, Anguilla

**Batting**

| M | I | NO | Runs | Av |
|---|---|---|---|---|
| 221 | 206 | 54 | 1814 | 11.93 |
| 50 | 100 | ct/st | | |
| 2 | - | 61 | | |

**Bowling**

| O | M | Runs | Wkts | Av |
|---|---|---|---|---|
| 6232.5 | 1312 | 19492 | 614 | 31.74 |
| 5wI | 10wM | | | |
| 18 | 4 | | | |

**Best Performances**
59 v. Surrey, The Oval, 1993
9/38 v. Gloucestershire, Southampton, 1996

A cheerful and hard-working opening bowler from Anguilla, Cardigan Connor was a popular figure on the Hampshire scene from 1984 to 1998. He was unusual among opening bowlers in that he seemed to get better as he got older. There were periodic high points early on: he had a productive first year when Malcolm Marshall was away with the West Indies, and an excellent season in 1989, taking 7 for 31 as Gloucestershire were dismissed for 48. After Marshall had retired, however, Connor came into his own as the County's spearhead, until persistent knee trouble forced his retirement.

Indeed, injury blighted the final few years of Connor's career. This was very frustrating for the County and the player because he had become a genuinely accomplished bowler. Wisden attributed the transformation from workaday County seamer to new-ball maestro to the emergence, in 1994, of a 'previously undiscovered outswinger'. He took 72 Championship wickets at 24.82 that year and on two occasions took 10 wickets in a match, something he had managed only once before. On the first day of the game v. Northamptonshire at Southampton, he bowled with what Wisden described as 'fire and accuracy' to take 7 for 47. In 1996, he was the County's leading wicket-taker, with 48 wickets at 21.52, secured in only 9 games in an injury-hit year. In Gloucestershire's first innings at Southampton, he took 9 for 38 – the last four in six balls – the best performance by any Hampshire bowler at Northlands Road. He finished seventh in the national bowling averages that year.

It was in this game though, in the second innings, that he suffered the breakdown that ended his season and, in retrospect at least, signalled the conclusion to his first-class career. He played in only a handful of Championship matches in the next two years, although he remained a force in one-day cricket. He settled the result of the second round NatWest game against Essex in 1998 in the first over of the day, dismissing Prichard, Hussain and Law at a cost of 2 runs.

Connor had always been a good one-day bowler, appearing in each of the County's one-day finals. Only Allan Donald and Geoff Arnold have taken more than his 80 wickets in the NatWest competition, and he is Hampshire's leading Sunday League wicket-taker. He was very reliable at 'the death'; best exemplified by his nerveless performance against Surrey in 1986. Surrey needed seven to win in the last over with four wickets left, but Connor denied them victory to ensure that Hampshire won the Sunday League title. He was an enthusiastic tail-ender, who showed a similarly cool frame of mind when in a Championship match against Gloucestershire in 1993, with two balls remaining, one wicket left and four needed to win, he straight drove a six.

**Born:** 16 October 1944, Cleethorpes, Lincs.

### Batting

| M | I | NO | Runs | Av |
|---|---|----|------|-----|
| 188 | 178 | 65 | 615 | 5.44 |
| 50 | 100 | ct/st | | |
| - | - | 84 | | |

### Bowling

| O | M | Runs | Wkts | Av |
|---|---|------|------|-----|
| 6185.2 | 1577 | 14354 | 693 | 20.71 |
| 5wI | 10wM | | | |
| 38 | 4 | | | |

### Best Performances
35 *v.* Somerset, Portsmouth, 1969
9/25 *v.* Lancashire, Manchester, 1965

When, in the mid-1960s, Hampshire could select a side including Derek Shackleton, David White and Bob Cottam, they must have had one of the strongest pace attacks in the history of County cricket. Taller than the other two, he bowled at a lively fast-medium pace and could be a real handful when conditions suited him. Armed with a natural outswinger he taught himself to bowl inswingers – in the wet summer of 1968, he cut down his pace and bowled off-cutters. For over a decade, he was one of the most accomplished pace bowlers in County cricket: his career average with Hampshire indicates his quality. Since his retirement as a player, he has been one of the country's leading bowling coaches.

In 1968, Cottam achieved something that no Hampshire player had done for twenty years: he took more wickets at a lower average than Derek Shackleton. Cottam's 128 wickets at 16.74 (with 5 wickets in an innings nine times) were sufficient to gain him selection for the ill-fated 'd'Oliveira' tour of South Africa that winter, which became the ill-fated tour of Pakistan, where he performed very creditably in the two Test matches in which he played.

Cottam also took over 100 wickets in 1967 and 1969; in the latter year, when, for the first time, he enjoyed regular use of the new ball, he took 5 or more wickets in an innings on eight occasions. His most memorable perfor-

mance for Hampshire came a few years earlier in 1965 at Old Trafford when he took 9 for 25 in Lancashire's first innings. All of these were achieved in a row after Shackleton took the first wicket. It remains the best analysis ever achieved by a Hampshire bowler. Curiously, in Lancashire's second innings, Cottam failed to take a wicket in thirteen overs, as Shackleton and White dismissed them for 107 and Hampshire won by 13 runs. Later in the year, against Kent at Canterbury, he took 10 for 74 in the match (6 for 38 and 4 for 36).

Cottam had made a very promising start as an eighteen year old in 1963. In only his second game, against Middlesex at Lord's, he bowled unchanged with Shackleton in the Middlesex first innings to take 5 for 74 and took 4 for 70 in the second, Hampshire winning by 99 runs. Against Leicestershire at Portsmouth, he took 6 for 10: Hampshire won by an innings, having scored 174 for 8.

After the three extremely good years of 1967, 1968 and 1969, Cottam's bowling seemed to lose something of its edge. There were times when he looked far from gruntled, and nobody was very surprised when he went off to Northamptonshire where a change of scene revived his career. He was unlucky in that almost uniquely among leading cricketers who played for Hampshire for any length of time between the mid-1950s and the mid-1990s, he failed to win a title with the County.

# Nigel Cowley

RHB, ROB, 1974-1989

**Born:** 1 March 1953, Shaftesbury, Dorset

**Batting**

| M | I | NO | Runs | Av |
|---|---|----|------|-----|
| 257 | 358 | 58 | 6773 | 22.57 |
| **50** | **100** | ct/st | | |
| 30 | 2 | 96 | | |

**Bowling**

| O | M | Runs | Wkts | Av |
|---|---|------|------|-----|
| 5127.1 | 1338 | 13979 | 425 | 32.89 |
| **5wI** | **10wM** | | | |
| 5 | - | | | |

**Best Performances**

109* v. Somerset, Taunton, 1977
6/48 v. Leicestershire, Southampton, 1982

Surely the best professional cricketer to have emerged from Dorset, Nigel Cowley was a resourceful and combative cricketer who played for Hampshire from 1974 to 1989. Below average height and chunkily built, 'Dougal' was a right-handed middle-order batsman and a bowler of rather flat, but economical off-spin, who was a particularly effective one-day player.

It was as a gutsy one-day batsman that Cowley first came to the fore, in a gripping Benson & Hedges semi-final at Northlands Road v. Gloucestershire in 1977. Chasing 181 to win, Hampshire were reeling at 18 for 4, a rampant Mike Procter having taken a hat-trick. Cowley then helped David Turner add 111 for the fifth wicket and went on to make the top score of 59. Hampshire lost to the eventual title winners by 7 runs.

At this stage in his career, Cowley was seen more as a batsman. In the one-day games, Hampshire tended to rely on their battery of seamers. In the Championship in that same year, 1977, he scored 687 runs at an average of 36, but took only 29 wickets at a cost of 38 each. Batting usually at five or six, he made a number of useful contributions including his highest score of 109 not out v. Somerset at Taunton: coming in at 89 for 4 (which soon became 91 for 6) he put on 92 for the seventh wicket with Mike Taylor and 135 for the ninth with Bob Stephenson. He was capped

the following year when he took 56 first-class wickets at 30.35.

Cowley was a fixture in both one-day and three-day sides for the next few years, and was always chipping in with useful performances. He was Hampshire's leading run-scorer and wicket-taker in the Sunday League in 1981 when they came sixth. He started the 1982 Championship season in fine style, scoring 104 and taking a career-best 6 for 48 v. Leicestershire in the first match of the season. The following year he took 41 wickets at 25.68 but made few runs, while in 1984 he completed 1,000 runs for the season at an average of 30 and took 56 first-class wickets at 31.26. Against Northamptonshire, he had a spell of 3 top-order wickets for 1 run.

In the following years, his Championship appearances were more limited, but he remained a vital member of the one-day side, scoring useful runs down the order and making telling contributions with his bowling. His miserly economy rate was critical in the early rounds of the Benson & Hedges Cup in 1988 and in the final itself. He conceded 17 runs in 11 overs for one wicket as well as running out John Morris, the only Derbyshire batsman to get a decent start.

Nigel Cowley played for Glamorgan in 1990. He is now a first-class umpire and his son, Darren, is a fine attacking left-handed batsman for Dorset.

# W.L.C. Creese
LHB, LM, 1928-1939

**Born:** 28 December 1907, Park Town,
   Transvaal, South Africa
**Died:** 9 March 1974, Dover, Kent

### Batting

| M | I | NO | Runs | Av |
|---|---|----|------|-----|
| 278 | 453 | 41 | 9894 | 24.01 |
| 50 | 100 | ct/st | | |
| 50 | 6 | 190 | | |

### Bowling

| O | M | Runs | Wkts | Av |
|---|---|------|------|-----|
| 4175.4 | 943 | 11141 | 401 | 27.78 |
| 5wI | 10wM | | | |
| 15 | 1 | | | |

### Best Performances
241 v. Northamptonshire, Northampton, 1939
8/37 v. Lancashire, Southampton, 1936

William Leonard Charles Creese came from a family which was for several generations connected with the administration of the Newlands ground at Cape Town. He came to England and qualified for Hampshire in 1928, after two years' residence. His early appearances for Hampshire were very tentative but in a few innings, he showed promise as a fast scorer – v. Sussex at Portsmouth in 1930 he scored 87 out of 157 in two hours, setting Sussex, who had had all the best of the match, what proved the impossible task of scoring 102 in eighty minutes. He played with more success in 1932 when his runs increased to 723, at 21.90, but his career really took off in the next season, when he exceeded one thousand runs for the first time and hit two centuries. The first was a remarkable performance which led to victory over Middlesex at Portsmouth by an innings and 119 runs; hitting no fewer than 24 fours, he batted only three-and-a-half hours for his 165 not out. He finished the season with a second hundred to stave off disaster v. Essex at Bournemouth.

A hard-hitting left-hander, he made most of his runs by hard drives and leg-side shots. From 1934, his bowling, fast-medium left hand, also played an increasingly important role in the County's success. He improved on his previous efforts to take 52 wickets in 1934 and 58 in 1935, while his average dropped to 24.16.

Then in 1936, he reached his high point

when he hit 1,331 runs at an average of 30.92 to head the batting averages, without once reaching three figures, and formed a formidable combination with the slower left-hander, Stuart Boyes, capturing 95 wickets at 22.93 each. He saved Hampshire from defeat by Surrey at the Oval in May following a first innings score of 58, with one of 94 not out accumulated in three hours and fifteen minutes; Boyes stayed with him for two hours while they added 110 runs. His outstanding feat with the ball came at the end of July at Southampton. After Boyes and Herman had put Lancashire out for 98 and gained Hampshire a first innings lead of 45, Creese suddenly became unplayable, turning the ball in bewildering fashion, to take 8 wickets in succession while only 13 runs were scored from his bowling. His final analysis was 21-6-37-8.

Injuries to both Boyes and Creese in 1937 meant that they hardly ever bowled in tandem. Len Creese's own form did not fall much below that of 1936, but he missed 11 championship matches, and his total of wickets fell to 57. Dick Moore's successors in the captaincy did not make as much use of Creese's bowling, but he remained among the most effective batsmen in the side and scored well over 1,000 runs in the last two seasons before the Second World War. He began the summer of 1939 in tremendous form, with 241 against Northants in the second game, but fell right away and struggled to achieve four figures by the end of the season.

Len Creese did not return to Hampshire, although he played for Combined Services in 1946 and subsequently for Dorset. He became groundsman at Hastings, and later for Sussex CCC at Hove, and so completed nearly fifty years in the first-class game.

# Desmond Eagar

RHB, SLA, 1946-1957

**Born:** 8 December 1917, Cheltenham, Gloucestershire
**Died:** 13 September 1977, Kingsbridge, Devon

**Batting**

| M | I | NO | Runs | Av |
|---|---|----|------|-----|
| 311 | 514 | 34 | 10091 | 21.02 |
| 50 | 100 | ct/st | | |
| 40 | 8 | 333 | | |

**Bowling**

| O | M | Runs | Wkts | Av |
|---|---|------|------|-----|
| 200.3 | 15 | 937 | 15 | 62.46 |
| 5wI | 10wM | | | |
| - | - | | | |

**Best Performances**
158* v. Oxford University, Oxford, 1954
2/10 v. Kent, Southampton, 1957

Several Counties have had one – somebody who devoted a lifetime not only as player but as administrator to their club until somehow they came to personify it. In the 'golden age' there were the aristocrats Lords Hawke and Harris of Yorkshire and Kent. Then there was John Daniell of Somerset and Brian Sellers, also of Yorkshire and, latterly, Wilf Wooller of Glamorgan and Trevor Bailey of Essex.

For Hampshire, it was Desmond Eagar. Like the others in this select group – except, perhaps, Bailey – Eagar was not a great player, although he was certainly a gifted sportsman. He was a hockey blue and wrote about the sport as well as his cricketing skill as a brilliant close fielder – he held 323 catches in his 311 matches for Hampshire mostly at short leg. But his contribution to Hampshire cricket cannot be measured in terms of runs and wickets. For over thirty years, Eagar simply was Hampshire cricket. Nothing happened without his approval – players came and went on his say-so. He put the county on the map and laboured tirelessly to increase membership. Much of the work was mundane and literally thankless. Doubtless he would have rolled the wicket and sold the scorecards if he had had to. When, twenty-three years after his death, the

bulldozers came to Northlands Road, if any one person's era had come to an end, it was Eagar's.

On the field, it was his captaincy and his fielding that made a difference. Appointed to lead the side and to be joint secretary in 1946 (ahead of the better known F.R. Brown) he had played a few games for Gloucestershire before the war and obtained a blue at Oxford in 1939 when he headed the University's averages, Eagar gradually developed a combination of returning old pro's and hopeful youngsters into an effective unit. Sixteenth in the table in 1947 and 1949 under Eagar's leadership, which was described as 'inspiring' in his *Wisden* obituary, Hampshire gradually got better and better. Fielding was something that Eagar always stressed. His early sides may have had frailties in batting or bowling, but he saw no reason why they should be defective in fielding. He was fortunate that even in his forties John Arnold remained a brilliant cover point, but everyone was exhorted to contribute. By 1953, Hampshire had become one of the youngest sides in the Championship and Eagar was able to mould them into a professional unit to take on the best.

In 1955, when Hampshire came third in the Championship, the highest they had ever achieved, the side was demonstrably Eagar's team. Only Leo Harrison had ever played for a Hampshire captain other than him. Eagar had been responsible for recruiting Roy Marshall, the West Indian opener whose batting made such a difference to Hampshire. He had discovered, one might almost say invented, Derek Shackleton. The County were so short of fast-bowling resources in 1949 that the professionals were asked to demonstrate their potential in the nets – Shackleton, hitherto a leg-spinner, had a go and was revealed as a natural, if not preternatural, seam bowler. Eagar also appointed Arthur Holt as coach. A moderately successful bats-

Desmond Eagar preferred aggression.

man in the years immediately before and after the war, Holt had been born to coach and the 1955 side, with significant contributions from 'Holt's Colts', owed much to his influence. But Eagar was the guiding hand. The 1955 side, with a couple of strategic additions from outside the county, became the 1961 side which won the Championship under Colin Ingleby-Mackenzie, himself hand-picked by his predecessor. They had in effect been joint captains in Eagar's last season, 1957.

By that time, Eagar's contribution as a batsman was negligible. He was an aggressive batsman in the middle order who never really did himself justice. John Arlott, writing in 1950, said that he had never had a sufficiently good run of scores to give himself confidence as a batsman. Nonetheless he reached 1,000 runs in a season five times and scored 990 in 1951. In the best amateur tradition, he was one of the last men to sport a Harlequin cap though rarely, it was said, north of the Trent.

Eagar's administrative skills were recognised when he was chosen to accompany the MCC side to Australia in 1958/59 as assistant manager.

He died in 1977, still very much in harness, at the age of just fifty-nine. His widow, Marjorie, is a life vice-president of the club and their son, Patrick, is the doyen of cricket photographers.

# Colonel James Fellowes

RHB, RFM, 1883-1885

**Born:** 25 August 1841, Cape of Good Hope, South Africa
**Died:** 3 May 1916, Dedham, Essex

**Batting**

| M | I | NO | Runs | Av |
|---|---|----|------|-----|
| 11 | 20 | 5 | 186 | 12.40 |
| **50** | **100** | **ct/st** | | |
| - | - | 17 | | |

**Bowling**

| O | M | Runs | Wkts | Av |
|---|---|------|------|-----|
| 136.1 | 81 | 393 | 11 | 35.72 |
| **5wl** | **10wM** | | | |
| - | - | | | |

**Best Performances**
26 v. Derbyshore, Derby, 1895
3/38 v. MCC, Southampton, 1885

James Fellowes was already aged forty-one when he played the first of his eleven matches for Hampshire in 1883, but he cannot be left out of any list of contributors to the success of the club. He shared the post of honorary secretary with Russell Bencraft in the 1880s, and it is thanks to his enthusiasm and determined negotiations with the Hulse Estate that the club obtained a year's lease of what became, from 1885, the county ground at Northlands Road. More than this, Fellowes was responsible for laying out the ground and for the construction of the first pavilion. Subsequently, the Hampshire County Cricket Ground Company was formed and the freehold purchased. Fellowes had been a formidable fast, round-arm bowler in Army cricket. Over the ten years up to 1883, he captured 836 wickets for the Royal Engineers. He was also a big

hitter, who once hit W.G. Grace for 20 runs, 2 sixes and 2 fours from a four-ball over. He also once hit a ball so hard onto his foot that he broke a toe! In nine matches for Kent and eleven for Hampshire between 1873 and 1885, he took 60 wickets in all at 18.98 each. A great innovator, he was the founder of the Hampshire Hogs CC which remains one of the principal clubs in the county. He subsequently moved to Devon, where he became secretary of the county cricket club, and founded the famous Devon Dumplings CC. He was honoured by being selected as one of eighteen veterans who played against MCC at Lord's in the club's centenary week in 1887. He was father-in-law of W.C. Hedley, who played first for Somerset and later for Hampshire, and was also a distinguished figure in Army cricket.

# Charles Burgess Fry

RHB, RFM, 1909-1921

**Born:** 25 April 1872, West Croydon
**Died:** 7 September 1956, Hampstead, London

## Batting

| M | I | NO | Runs | Av |
|---|---|---|---|---|
| 44 | 72 | 7 | 3829 | 58.90 |
| 50 | 100 | ct/st | | |
| 15 | 14 | 27 | | |

## Bowling

| O | M | Runs | Wkts | Av |
|---|---|---|---|---|
| 5 | 1 | 19 | 0 | - |
| 5wI | 10wM | | | |
| - | - | | | |

## Best Performances

258* *v.* Gloucestershire, Southampton, 1911

For some reason, C.B. Fry has not been made as much of in Hampshire as his standing as a sportsman would permit. He was already thirty-seven years old when he joined the County, and he never played a full season for the side yet, in his 44 matches, he scored over 3,800 runs, at an average of nearly 59. It was also while he was associated with the County that he led England to victory in the tests in the Triangular Tournament *v.* Australia and South Africa in 1912. Fry had enjoyed a wonderful career with Sussex between 1894 and 1908. In 1900, he had crafted a hundred and a double hundred in a game with Surrey, and the next year scored 3,147 runs, an aggregate which had been exceeded only by his Sussex colleague, Ranjitsinhji in 1899. His 13 hundreds in 1901 remained a record until 1925 when Jack Hobbs beat it. In 1901 he also hit 6 hundreds in successive innings.

However, partly because of his attachment to the training ship *Mercury* on the River Hamble, east of Southampton, Fry never showed the dedication to county cricket with Hampshire that he had given for so many seasons to Sussex. When he did play, his performances showed little decline – in 1911, his record in all matches shows: 26 innings, 2 not out, 1,728 runs, highest innings 258*, average 72.00. For Hampshire that season, his 6 hundreds, made in 18 innings, included one in each innings *v.* Kent at Canterbury, and 258 not out in the game with Gloucestershire at Southampton. In that innings, powerful driving, clever placing to leg, and accurate cutting, brought him one five and 34 fours. It is somehow typical of his insouciance that he did not play for the County again that season.

In 1921, amid speculation that he would again be selected to captain England against Australia, he appeared in many of the early fixtures, scoring with much of his old fluency, notably in his 96 against Kent, but he suggested that Tennyson should take over the England captaincy when a replacement for Johnnie Douglas was needed, and soon after he broke a finger and did not play English cricket again. His last match of first-class cricket came in India the following winter and after that his life was dispersed among a variety of activities: presiding at the *Mercury*, unsuccessful candidacy for Parliament, a period of breakdown, cricket writing and other journalism, until at last he became a grand old man and one of the earliest subjects of *This is Your Life*.

# Richard Gilliat

LHB, 1966-1978

**Born:** 20 May 1944, Wale, Herts

**Batting**

| M | I | NO | Runs | Av |
|---|---|---|---|---|
| 220 | 351 | 40 | 9358 | 30.09 |
| 50 | 100 | ct/st | | |
| 49 | 16 | 181 | | |

**Bowling**

| O | M | Runs | Wkts | Av |
|---|---|---|---|---|
| 17 | 1 | 133 | 3 | 44.33 |
| 5wI | 10wM | | | |
| - | - | | | |

**Best Performances**

223* v. Warwickshire, Southampton, 1969
1/3 v. Kent, Southampton, 1973

An outstanding sportsman at Charterhouse and Oxford, where he obtained blues at soccer as well as cricket, Richard Gilliat could justly claim to have been Hampshire's most successful captain.

As a batsman he had a talent that is not reflected in his career figures. Initially, he seemed a rather dour player but in his second full County season (1969), he was hit on the head by a ball from Keith Boyce of Essex. Recovering from this blow he seemed to become a different sort of batsman, completing a century in a much more aggressive manner than previously and continuing in the same vein as a forceful left-hander although he could be gritty and obdurate when the occasion demanded. He finished the season with 1,348 runs at an average of 40, with 6 centuries, including a career-bent 223 not out v. Warwickshire and was spoken of as a Test candidate.

He missed nearly the whole of 1970 through injury. In 1971,therefore, he had to justify his place in the team as well as establish his authority as the newly-appointed captain of a side which included his predecessor. Gilliat struggled with the bat initially but ultimately more than held his own as a batsman throughout the good years that followed. In those years from 1973 to 1975 he shared many valuable partnerships with fellow left-hander David Turner.

Gilliat was an unselfish captain. He started the 1971 season, which was crucial for him, in his preferred position of first-wicket down, but moved to number 4 to accommodate Turner; in 1975 he dropped down again for Trevor Jesty.

Nobody could have expected Hampshire to win the Championship in 1973. They had a world-class opening batsman with a highly promising partner and a solid middle order, but it is, generally, bowlers who win matches and Hampshire's attack looked modest. Gilliat marshalled the apparently slender resources splendidly, led the side shrewdly, created great team spirit and fielded well, holding 23 catches, mostly at mid-off.

In 1974 Hampshire looked even better, with Andy Roberts leading the attack. But they failed to win any of their last five games, and the final match of that campaign, at Dean Park, v. Yorkshire (who were doubtless still moaning about having been cheated of the title in 1961) was abandoned, with Hampshire finishing second, two points behind Worcestershire.

In 1975, they finished third as injuries took their toll, but they won the Sunday League, the County's first one-day title. There followed three difficult years, culminating in the departure in the middle of 1978 of Barry Richards and Roberts. Despite this, the team won the Sunday League for the second time, a deeply satisfying victory for all concerned, with Gilliat leading from the front and opening the batting with Gordon Greenidge in the last five crucial games of the campaign. With the side much as he had found it, in a transitional phase, Gilliat then retired, first to the city and subsequently returned to Charterhouse.

# David Gower
LHB, 1990-1993

**Born:** 1 April 1957, Tunbridge Wells

## Batting
| M | I | NO | Runs | Av |
|---|---|---|---|---|
| 73 | 120 | 14 | 4325 | 40.80 |
| **50** | **100** | **ct/st** | | |
| 23 | 7 | 54 | | |

## Bowling
| O | M | Runs | Wkts | Av |
|---|---|---|---|---|
| 0.1 | 0 | 4 | 0 | - |
| **5wI** | **10wM** | | | |
| - | - | | | |

## Best Performances
155 v. Yorkshire, Basingstoke, 1992

It was noted in the commentary on Hampshire in the 1994 *Wisden* that David Gower, who retired from first-class cricket in 1993, had under achieved for Hampshire, although it was conceded, graciously and truly enough, that spectators would miss his artistry as a stroke-player. The same point was made, rather gratuitously – and without the bit about his artistry – in 1995. It is not entirely clear what is meant by 'under achieve' in this context. If the Hampshire committee in 1990 were under the impression that their new signing was going to bat for them as though every County game had the intensity of a Test match then they had been, like Rick going to Casablanca 'for the waters', misinformed.

As a Leicestershire player for fifteen years, Gower finished with a career average of 38. In four years with Hampshire he scored just over 4,000 runs at an average of just over 40 so the 'under achiever' point seems a little harsh. As a player on the big stage, Gower was exceptional, maintaining a Test average of well over 40 from the beginning of his career to the end. Almost certainly the most gifted English batsman of his generation, he had a huge following that was not limited to regular cricket watchers. But by a quirk of sporting celebrity, it was Gower's fate to be exasperating as well as exhilarating, and it is a moot point whether he exasperated his admirers (except those for whom he could do no wrong, who tended not to be Leicestershire or Hampshire supporters) more than his detractors.

County cricket was not, on the whole, a big enough stage for Gower, except for one-off events such as Lord's finals. As it happened, Hampshire, having had one of these in the previous 27 years, had two of them during Gower's four years with the County and his finest hour with the County was to be captain on the day they beat Surrey at Lord's in the 1991 NatWest final.

Much of Gower's time with Hampshire was over-shadowed by what became almost a national obsession with whether or not he ought to have been playing for England instead. Although supporters were often disappointed – in 1991 his highest score was 80 not out and he scored one century in 1992 – Gower played some marvellous innings for the county. He started with a hundred in his first game in 1990 and finished in a blaze of glory in 1993, while England were stumbling towards a humiliating defeat against Australia. The end was pure Gower: a dispute with the County about whether he could miss the start of the 1994 season to do media work in the West Indies. The County stood firm. Gower retired. He was thirty-seven.

# Jimmy Gray

RHB, RFM, 1948-1966

**Born:** 19 May 1926, Southampton

**Batting**

| M | I | NO | Runs | Av |
|---|---|----|------|----|
| 453 | 809 | 81 | 22450 | 30.83 |
| **50** | **100** | **ct/st** | | |
| 119 | 30 | 350 | | |

**Bowling**

| O | M | Runs | Wkts | Av |
|---|---|------|------|----|
| 5439.2 | 1522 | 13543 | 451 | 30.02 |
| **5wI** | **10wM** | | | |
| 11 | 1 | | | |

**Best Performances**

213* v. Derbyshire, Portsmouth, 1962
7/52 v. Glamorgan, Swansea, 1955

Jimmy Gray was one of three senior players in the Championship-winning side of 1961 (Leo Harrison and Derek Shackleton were the others) who had already established themselves before Desmond Eagar led the team to third place in 1955.

As John Arlott said, Gray was the very model of a modern professional cricketer: immaculately turned out, a neat and orthodox batsman, guaranteed to make his thousand-plus runs a year, a tidy medium-pace in-swing bowler always chipping in with useful wickets (he sometimes opened the bowling in his younger days) and a safe slip fielder. He was born and raised in Southampton and made his debut in 1948. He started as a middle-order batsman, but moved up to open in 1952, after the retirement of Neil McCorkell, occasionally moving down again to accommodate the amateurs David Blake and the Reverend J.R. Bridger. In 1953, he was the county's leading run scorer with 1,663 runs at 33.87 including 3 centuries and 10 other scores of over fifty. He also took 64 wickets at 23.81. In 1955, when Hampshire came third, Gray had one of his least successful years with the bat – Roy Marshall, whose first season it was, later acknowledged that his rapid scoring rate compelled Gray to adjust his style of play – but he took 50 wickets at 20.50, including a career best 7 for 52 against Glamorgan.

For nine years from 1955 to 1963 Gray opened the Hampshire batting with Marshall. They were an ideal combination. An evocative picture of them walking out to open an innings at the County Ground appeared in the 1962 *Hampshire Handbook*, aptly captioned 'Craftsman and Genius'. On 33 occasions, Marshall and Gray put on a century opening stand together for Hampshire including the then county record of 249 against Middlesex in 1960.

Like Marshall and Henry Horton, Gray was at his peak as a batsman in the years from 1958 to 1962. The latter year was his most successful statistically, with 2,224 runs at 40.43 including his highest score of 213 not out against Derbyshire – he scored 84 not out in the second innings. The following year, however, saw a drastic reversal of form and his worst return since 1950. He played on as a part-timer when he was settling into his second career as a schoolmaster, doing well in 1964, batting mostly in the middle order and finally retiring in 1966. Only three batsmen, none of them Hampshire-born, have scored more runs for the County than Gray.

A sensible and straightforward man, Gray kept a firm hand on the tiller as chairman of the County's cricket committee from 1988 to 1997.

# Gordon Greenidge
RHB, RFM, 1970-1987

**Born:** 1 May 1951, Black Bless, St Peter, Barbados

### Batting
| M | I | NO | Runs | Av |
|---|---|---|---|---|
| 275 | 472 | 35 | 19840 | 45.40 |
| **50** | **100** | **ct/st** | | |
| 100 | 48 | 315 | | |

### Bowling
| O | M | Runs | Wkts | Av |
|---|---|---|---|---|
| 124 | 29 | 387 | 16 | 24.18 |
| **5wI** | **10wM** | | | |
| 1 | - | | | |

### Best Performances
259 v. Sussex, Southampton, 1975
5/49 v. Surrey, Southampton, 1971

Of Hampshire's great post-war players, Gordon Greenidge – born in Barbados but brought up in Reading – is the most enigmatic. There is little doubt that after his arrival in England he did not have an easy time of it, yet his batting in his early years for Hampshire – full of drives, cuts and hooks hit by one of the most forceful strikers of a cricket ball – and his brilliant and exuberant fielding seemed to be an expression of extravagant power and vitality. By the 1980s he was established as one of the world's outstanding batsmen, but he sometimes cut a moody and introspective figure. 'Very difficult' was Mark Nicholas's considered view after Greenidge had left the county. A persistent knee strain plagued him in later years and it might have been expected to limit his effectiveness at the crease but instead, the appearance of the 'Greenidge limp' seemed to be the harbinger of a more than usually devastating assault on the bowling.

He played a few games for Hampshire batting in the middle order in 1970 and established himself as an opener the following year. He contributed mightily to Hampshire's Championship title in 1973, scoring more runs and centuries at a higher average than Barry Richards, with 5 centuries and 3 other scores of over 90. Of course, Greenidge was a beneficiary in these early years too: who can quantify the advantages gleaned from spend-

ing seven years as Barry Richards' opening partner? When Richards left in the middle of 1978, Greenidge effectively carried the Hampshire batting with Trevor Jesty, until the emergence of Chris Smith and Nicholas in the early 1980s.

Towards the end of 1975 he made Hampshire's highest score since the war (until it was eclipsed by John Crawley's 272 in 2002), 259 against an admittedly below par Sussex attack. It might not have been Greenidge's best innings, but it was a truly memorable one, containing 13 sixes (in the previous year his 273 for D.H. Robins' XI against the Pakistanis had also contained 13 sixes) and 24 fours with each landmark from 50 to 200 being reached with a six. He played some similarly pulverising one-day innings. He holds the Hampshire record for the highest individual score in each of the three one-day competitions – his 172 against Surrey in the Sunday League in 1987, when he put on 217 for the fourth wicket with Chris Smith, came off 142 balls and contained 10 sixes and 13 fours. When he made 177 v. Glamorgan in the Gillette Cup in 1975 (still the third-highest score against a first-class county in that competition), he and Richards put on 210 for the first wicket.

He was the last Hampshire batsman to score 2,000 runs in a season, finishing top of the national averages in 1986 with 2,035 runs at 67.85 with 8 centuries and 6 other scores of

over fifty. He ended the season in prodigious form: 222 (out of 338 for 2) *v.* Northamptonshire; 103 (out of 176 for 2) and 180 not out (out of 257 for 2 in 52.1 overs) *v.* Derbyshire. Hampshire won both games; and 126 and 30 against Sussex. In 1978, he scored 3 hundreds in successive innings. Greenidge scored 2 hundreds in a match three times for Hampshire – only Philip Mead has equalled that. He scored 5 double centuries for the County. Five times, twice on the first day, he scored one hundred or more runs in the first session of a day's play.

In 1987 he scored over 700 runs in eleven first-class matches, as well as a marvellous hundred in the MCC Bicentenary Match at Lord's. It was a surprise to many Hampshire supporters when it was announced that he would not be returning to the county after the 1988 West Indies tour of England. He was thirty-nine in 1989, but he was still good enough to score a double century in a Test match for the West Indies a year or so later: they have, to date, been unable to replace him successfully. When Hampshire took the decision to let him go, a county career of rare distinction ended on a decidedly flat, if not a sour note.

Gordon Greenidge's last appearance at the County Ground for the West Indies was in a one-day game *v.* Hampshire in 1988. He scored 103 with 8 sixes.

# Canon John Glennie Greig CIE
RHB, ROB, 1901-1922

**Born:** 24 October 1871, Mhon, India
**Died:** 24 May 1958, Milford, Surrey

## Batting
| M | I | NO | Runs | Av |
|---|---|----|------|-----|
| 77 | 137 | 9 | 4375 | 34.17 |

| 50 | 100 | ct/st | | |
|----|-----|-------|---|---|
| 17 | 10 | 52 | | |

## Bowling
| O | M | Runs | Wkts | Av |
|---|---|------|------|-----|
| 600.3 | 73 | 2050 | 64 | 32.03 |

| 5wI | 10wM | | | |
|-----|------|---|---|---|
| 4 | - | | | |

## Best Performances
249* v. Lancashire, Liverpool, 1901
6/38 v. Derbyshire, Southampton, 1901

'Junglie' Greig had two separate careers in cricket, in addition to his three consecutive careers off the field as soldier, secretary to the county cricket club, and Roman Catholic priest. His county cricket for Hampshire spread over eight seasons between 1901 and 1922, although he first appeared in first-class cricket v. Oxford and Cambridge Universities in 1897. In India, his birthplace, where his nickname came from the locals' pronunciation of his Christian names, he had excelled at cricket from the time of his arrival there as junior officer in 1893. Season after season he played in the Bombay Presidency matches against the Parsis, and later against the Hindus and Muslims, and in those matches, the highest grade of cricket in India, he was regarded as head and shoulders above his colleagues, who included R.M. Poore and many other players well known in county cricket. His larger scores included 184 not out, 142 and 204 v. the Oxford University Authentics touring side of 1902/03, which included several famous players. So when he first played for Hampshire at the age of twenty-nine, in 1901, he was already a very experienced player. In his third match for the County, he scored 119 against the South Africans (one of three centuries in the innings) and a few weeks later he played great cricket v. Lancashire at Liverpool: in the first innings he

was undefeated for 47, in the second (after Lancashire had replied with over 400 runs) he saved Hampshire from defeat with a magnificent innings of 249 not out. Although missed twice, his innings was described by *Wisden* as superb and his late cutting as quite a marvel of safety and brilliance: he was at the wicket for 5 hours and 20 minutes to save the match, hitting a five and 32 fours. He hit 3 other hundreds and finished with 1,277 runs, at an average of 41.19.

In the Derbyshire match at Southampton, he took with his slows 6 wickets for 38 and 9 for 106 in the match, but he bowled very little in subsequent years. He was not seen again in county cricket until 1905, when he averaged 50 for his 804 runs: in 1906, a fairly full season brought him 867 runs at 26 an innings: he made further successful forays for the county in 1910, 1914, 1920 and 1921. Harry Altham wrote of him, 'though slight of build and gentle of manner, there was in him a hard core that came out at the crease where his fine eye and wrists of steel made him one of the most attractive players in the country … as with an earlier Hampshire hero, Beldham, his peculiar glory was the cut …"

In 1922, he began an eight-year term as secretary of Hampshire. Then he trained for the Roman Catholic priesthood, and it was as the Revd Canon J.G. Greig that he served as president of Hampshire in 1945/46.

43

# Leo Harrison

RHB, WKT, 1939-1966

**Born:** 5 June 1922, Mudeford, Hants

**Batting**

| M | I | NO | Runs | Av |
|---|---|---|---|---|
| 387 | 593 | 100 | 8708 | 17.66 |
| **50** | **100** | ct/st | | |
| 27 | 6 | 567/99 | | |

**Bowling**

| O | M | Runs | Wkts | Av |
|---|---|---|---|---|
| 42.4 | 6 | 166 | 0 | - |
| **5wI** | **10wM** | | | |
| - | - | | | |

**Best Performance**
153 v. Nottinghamshire, Bournemouth, 1952

Leo Harrison had to work very hard and exercise enormous patience to establish his place in the County team. He had to wrestle with conversion from left-hand bat to right hand, and playing without glasses for years before he realised he needed them, but working a lengthy apprenticeship was a highly-gifted cricketer and a man of enormous spirit. Born at Mudeford, Christchurch, which is now in Dorset, Leo showed great promise as a small boy, joined the ground staff at sixteen, and he first appeared in the County side just before the outbreak of the Second World War. He appeared in the 1939 team photograph – just draped in the back left-hand corner, and he justified his selection showing determined defence when most of his seniors failed to do their bit. On his debut against Worcestershire, his scores were only 9 and 12, but only four of the others achieved double figures in each innings. Against the might of Yorkshire, whose attack included three current or future England bowlers, in the second innings, he was the only batsman to reach double figures, apart from Sam Pothecary, who made 61.

After six long years in the Army, Leo Harrison resumed his place in the Hampshire team in 1946, and he played a good deal over the next four years. In 1947, he scored over 500 runs in a full season: the next year he fared only half as well: then he was in and out of the side. Finally, in 1951, he took to wearing spectacles while batting. The outcome was

gratifying, as Leo established himself and earned his county cap. He already had a reputation as a superb fielder, in the covers for preference, but excelling everywhere. Now he became a leading batsman. He hit two centuries in his aggregate of 1,189 runs: next year he had three scores over three figures in the season's total of 1,191, the highest being 153 v. Nottinghamshire at Bournemouth.

Early in 1954, Leo took over the position of wicketkeeper as well as scoring 822 runs, a figure bettered by only two members of the side. By 1955, good judges regarded him as among the best wicketkeepers in the country and he was selected for the Players v. the Gentlemen at Lord's. John Arlott thought that the finest part of his wicketkeeping was in taking Derek Shackleton, for Shack, more than any of his contemporaries, constantly made the ball move late off the pitch. In 1959, his victims numbered 83 with 76 caught and 7 stumped. From 1955, his batting became only a secondary thing, although at number 8 he often played fluently, indeed elegantly, when quick runs were needed.

Again, John Arlott wrote of him, 'he is wise in cricket and shrewd about people. Honest as the day and a trier to the last gasp himself, he finds it hard to forgive anything which is not straight, or any cricket played with less than full effort. Know Leo Harrison and you must trust him and like him.'

# Matthew Hayden

LHB, 1997

**Born:** 29 October 1971, Kingaroy

### Batting

| M | I | NO | Runs | Av |
|---|---|----|------|-----|
| 17 | 30 | 3 | 1446 | 53.55 |

| 50 | 100 | ct/st | | |
|----|-----|-------|---|---|
| 7 | 4 | 13 | | |

### Bowling

| O | M | Runs | Wkts | Av |
|---|---|------|------|-----|
| 33 | 0 | 166 | 3 | 55.33 |

| 5wI | 10wM | | | |
|-----|------|---|---|---|
| - | - | | | |

### Best Performances

235* v. Warwickshire, Southampton, 1997
2/17 v. Sussex, Southampton, 1997

Matthew Hayden, the left-handed opener for Queensland and Australia, spent only one summer in 1997 with Hampshire, but that was sufficient for him to make a significant impact in the county. Few Hampshire supporters will have been surprised at Hayden's emergence in the last year or so as one of the leading batsmen in Test cricket.

A tall and muscular man with broad shoulders and strong convictions, Hayden's Hampshire sojourn coincided, rather pointedly, with an Ashes tour of England for which another left-handed opener, Matthew Elliott, had been preferred to him. Elliott proceeded to have the best series of his career but if Hayden – who had toured in 1993, making a century at Northlands Road – found this disheartening, he certainly did not show it.

He started modestly, making only 150 runs in his first seven first-class innings for the county but he put any troubles behind him in a high-scoring draw v. Warwickshire at Southampton, making 235 not out, with 1 six and 30 fours, in the first innings, followed by 119 in the second. In the following game v. Derbyshire he made 46 and 136 not out, putting on 213 for the first wicket with Jason Laney. After a quiet game v. Somerset at Basingstoke he made 150 at Northampton, according to *Wisden*, one of the best innings played at the ground in recent years. (Hayden went on to have two very successful seasons with Northamptonshire.)

Some people, however, are never satisfied and this purple patch was being constructed against a backdrop of mutterings from some Hampshire supporters to the effect that the County's admittedly woeful start to the season could have been avoided if, among other things, they had signed a bowler as overseas player rather than a batsman. This seemed, to say the least, a little harsh on Hayden, who was to finish the Championship season with 1,438 runs at an average of 57.52 and although Robin Smith, Giles White and Laney all had respectable seasons, none of them reached 900 runs in the Championship. Hayden also scored almost a thousand one-day runs. More to the point, the committee would no doubt have signed an overseas bowler had one been available. Hampshire's previous overseas player, fast bowler Winston Benjamin, had conspicuously under-achieved. It was clear that a change would have to be made for the following year and Hayden bowed out with a remarkably successful Hampshire career behind him.

# George Heath ———————————————
RHB, RFM, 1937-1949

**Born:** 20 February 1913, The Peak, Hong Kong
**Died:** 6 March 1994, Fareham, Hants

**Batting**

| M | I | NO | Runs | Av |
|---|---|----|------|-----|
| 132 | 188 | 83 | 586 | 5.58 |
| 50 | 100 | ct/st | | |
| - | - | 49 | | |

**Bowling**

| O | M | Runs | Wkts | Av |
|---|---|------|------|-----|
| 4161 | 731 | 11359 | 404 | 28.11 |
| 5wI | 10wM | | | |
| 23 | 2 | | | |

**Best Performances**
34* v. Lancashire, Southampton, 1939
7/49 v. Derbyshire, Portsmouth, 1947

In the mid-1930s, Hampshire were looking to replace a generation of great bowlers. Between them, Alec Kennedy, Jack Newman and George Brown took over 5,000 wickets for the County and while 'Lofty' Herman was able to open at one end, he needed a regular partner.

George Heath was born in Hong Kong but as a young man played in the Bournemouth area. He was a quick away-swing bowler of whom John Arlott wrote that 'He was not strong defensively after the ball had ceased to swing, but as a shock opening bowler he was very high quality indeed.'

George Heath first played for Hampshire's Club & Ground in 1935 at the age of twenty-two. He made his Championship debut in 1937 v. Essex at Portsmouth and by the end of that year he had taken 67 wickets. He and 'Lofty' formed an opening partnership that served Hampshire well in the next season and for three years after the war, before Shackleton, Carty and Cannings replaced the veteran pace-men. We can only wonder what they might have achieved with the six seasons at the height of their experience and power, although the odd circumstance of Herman's single season in the Lancashire League broke the partnership in 1939.

In that year Heath was asked to do too much on his own and took just 57 wickets, but in 1938 he had managed 97 at 23.77 each including 7-89 v. Kent at Southampton in the traditional Whitsun match, with Hampshire winning by 8 wickets. Wisden felt that he came close to selection for England in that season.

After the war, he took 41 wickets in 1946 and in that great batsmen's summer of 1947, 76 wickets at 31.11. They included 7-49 bowling unchanged in the first innings v. Derbyshire at Portsmouth (13-152 in the match). Hampshire won this match thanks also to a magnificent unbroken partnership of 163 in under two hours by McCorkell and Eagar.

After this, Heath rather fell away with 38 wickets in 1948 and 16 in 1949 when he retired. The Hampshire Handbook recorded that he and 'Lofty' had 'given great and unselfish service' and 'will be missed'. Two years later, the club granted George a testimonial. He had played 132 games for the County and finished his career with more than 400 wickets.

George Heath died in 1994, although his death was not reported in either Wisden or The Hampshire Handbook until 2002.

# Malcolm Heath

RFM, LHB, 1954-1962

**Born:** 9 March 1934, Bournemouth

**Batting**

| M | I | NO | Runs | Av |
|-----|-----|------|------|------|
| 143 | 163 | 66 | 569 | 5.86 |
| 50 | 100 | ct/st | | |
| - | - | 42 | | |

**Bowling**

| O | M | Runs | Wkts | Av |
|------|------|-------|------|-------|
| 4831 | 1095 | 13237 | 527 | 25.11 |
| 5wI | 10wM | | | |
| 18 | 5 | | | |

**Best Performances**
33 v. Sussex, Portsmouth, 1955
8/43 v. Sussex, Portsmouth, 1958

Malcolm Heath was an exceptionally tall, fast-medium bowler who enjoyed one very successful year with Hampshire. He made many other useful contributions, especially in 1955, when the County came third in the Championship, and in 1961, when they were top. However, for Heath, the outstanding performance came in 1958, when they finished second.

Heath's height enabled him to generate extra bounce and he could be genuinely hostile, although it has been said that a lack of ruthlessness and a benign temperament prevented him from realising his full potential. At the start of his career, his path to a regular place had been blocked in that, in Derek Shackleton and Vic Cannings, Hampshire had one of the most highly respected pairs of opening bowlers in the country. Jimmy Gray could also provide useful back-up without distorting the balance of the side. Nonetheless, in only eight games in 1955, Heath took 33 wickets at 20.45. In 1957 he was the County's second highest wicket-taker, with 76 at 27.06 in 21 games, and was awarded his cap.

In 1958, though, Heath was a revelation. Opening regularly with Shackleton – Cannings was often absent through injury – he took 126 first-class wickets at 16.42 and on ten occasions he took five or more wickets in an innings. Hampshire had to wait until their fourth game for their first win, v. Worcester-shire, Heath taking 5 for 28 in the second innings. A few weeks later, he and Shackleton destroyed Glamorgan at Neath for 72 and 46, Heath taking 7 for 46 and 3 for 21. The two of them bowled unchanged through the match, save for one over by Mervyn Burden. Three weeks later v. Sussex at Portsmouth, Heath took 5 for 43 and a career-best 8 for 43. Hampshire went to Burton-upon-Trent in mid-August as Championship leaders. After a rain interrupted first day, 39 wickets fell on the second. Heath achieved, with Shackleton, the rare feat, so narrowly missed at Neath, of bowling unchanged through two completed innings of a match as Derbyshire were bowled out for 74 and 107, Heath taking 6 for 35 and 7 for 52. However, Hampshire, who were themselves dismissed for 23 and 55, lost and the title eluded them.

Bowlers generally had a harder time of it in the exceptionally fine summer of 1959 and although Heath took 71 wickets, second to Shackleton for Hampshire, they cost 34.84 apiece. Cannings retired at the end of that year, but the role of Shackleton's opening partner was assumed by David White. Heath continued to put in useful performances taking 74 first-class wickets in 1960 and 54 wickets in 15 games in 1961.

Malcolm Heath has spent his life after leaving Hampshire in cricket, playing League in the north of England and coaching.

# Oswald William 'Lofty' Herman
RFM, RHB, 1929-1948

**Born:** 18 September 1907, Horsepath, Oxford
**Died:** 24 June 1987, Southampton

**Batting**

| M | I | NO | Runs | Av |
|---|---|---|---|---|
| 321 | 495 | 105 | 4327 | 11.09 |
| 50 | 100 | ct/st | | |
| 10 | - | 120 | | |

**Bowling**

| O | M | Runs | Wkts | Av |
|---|---|---|---|---|
| 9378.3 | 1647 | 28137 | 1041 | 27.02 |
| 5wI | 10wM | | | |
| 58 | 6 | | | |

**Best Performances**
92 v. Leicestershire, Leicester, 1948
8/49 v. Yorkshire, Bournemouth, 1930

Oswald William Herman was known as 'Lofty' throughout his cricket career for the most obvious of reasons. He was born in Cowley in 1907 and was one of a number of Oxfordshire men who journeyed south in the first half of the century to pursue a professional career.

'Lofty' had the physical attributes of an opening bowler and after a trial on the recommendation of Bowell, he came into the side in 1929 for Hampshire's fifth match v. Glamorgan at Swansea. Kennedy, Newman and Boyes were the main bowlers as Hampshire won by 41 runs and he had to wait until the next match (v. Gloucestershire) to claim his first wicket. In those first two matches he scored 0-1-0-0*, and with 1-78, he was replaced by the amateurs F.A. Gross and H.R. Sprinks.

He returned on 19 June and, opening the bowling for the first time, took six Glamorgan wickets in the first innings as Hampshire won again. Ten days later, he improved on this with 6-73 v. Surrey and he was established as an opening bowler alongside Alec Kennedy. He finished his first season with 53 wickets at 25 apiece. He was predominantly an inswing bowler with good pace off the pitch.

The following year was Jack Newman's last, Alex Kennedy was thirty-nine but the youthful Herman took fewer wickets (37), although he recorded the best figures of his career, 8-49 v. Yorkshire at Bournemouth. In 1931, he came back with 57 wickets, and in 1932, 94 at 23.12 each. His best bowling in that year was 4-51 and 7-50 in a big victory v. Essex when he also scored 38 for once out. By 1936 and 1937, he was Hampshire's leading pace bowler and took 7

wickets in an innings on five occasions in those two years. In 1938, he took a top-order hat-trick against Glamorgan at Portsmouth and finished the season with 101 wickets.

Despite this success, he left Hampshire and spent one season in the Lancashire League in 1939. In 1945, he returned to play in a number of friendly matches and took his place in the Championship side when the competition resumed in 1946. He sometimes bowled more slowly after the war and took over 100 wickets yet again in that first season, but he fell away dramatically in 1947, dismissing just 37 batsmen as Vic Ransom often opened the bowling. In the following year, he almost doubled that total and took 8-75 v. Gloucestershire at Bournemouth after both first innings had been dominated by the spinners, Bailey, Knott, Goddard and Cook. In late summer, Hampshire provided the forty year old with a new partner, Derek Shackleton, and while 'Lofty' was still available in 1949 and was top wicket-taker for the Second XI, he did not play for the County as 'Shack' took 100 wickets for the first of 20 consecutive seasons. 'Lofty' retired at the end of that season, finishing as one of only seven players to pass 1,000 first-class wickets for Hampshire.

Lofty went on to play for Wiltshire and acted as coach at Oxford University before becoming a first-class umpire. His son, Bob, helped to bowl Hampshire to their second Championship in 1973.

# Bob Herman
RFM, RHB, 1972-1977

**Born:** 30 November 1946, Southampton

**Batting**

| M | I | NO | Runs | Av |
|---|---|---|---|---|
| 89 | 92 | 17 | 869 | 11.58 |
| 50 | 100 | ct/st | | |
| 1 | - | 32 | | |

**Bowling**

| O | M | Runs | Wkts | Av |
|---|---|---|---|---|
| 2769 | 747 | 6768 | 270 | 25.06 |
| 5wI | 10wM | | | |
| 8 | - | | | |

**Best Performances**
56 *v.* Worcestershire, Worcester, 1972
8/42 *v.* Warwickshire, Portsmouth, 1972

However optimistic Bob Herman felt when moving to Hampshire from Middlesex in 1972, it is improbable that even in his wildest dreams he could have contemplated leading the county's bowling attack to Championship glory only a year later; yet that is precisely what happened.

It was the bowlers who won Hampshire the Championship in 1973 with the genial and hard-working Herman as the opening bowler and Mike Taylor, the leading wicket-taker, with 63 at 23.76. He also bowled more overs than anyone else. A fast-medium bowler with the ability to move the ball away from the right-handed batsman, persistence and accuracy were the hallmarks of Herman's bowling that year. In the first Championship game of the season he took 5 for 49 *v.* Leicestershire which was the only time he took five wickets in a Championship match that year but he rarely failed to take two or three or four, often at the top of the order and his value to the team effort was immense.

Herman arrived at Hampshire at a time when the county's pace-bowling resources were looking decidedly threadbare, Bob Cottam having left for Northamptonshire. Herman had spent seven seasons with Middlesex without establishing himself. There was, of course, a link with the county – his father 'Lofty' had done yeoman service for Hampshire in the years spanning the war and Herman had been born in the county.

It would be interesting to know who was more impressed – Hampshire, Middlesex or the bowler himself – by Herman's response to the opportunity he had been given: 81 wickets at 21.66? Peter Sainsbury was the next highest wicket-taker with 49. He must have enjoyed his return to Lord's taking 4 for 80 and 5 for 47 as Hampshire won by 5 wickets. Shortly afterwards he took a career-best 8 for 42 against Warwickshire in 32.3 overs.

1974 was always going to be interesting with Andy Roberts leading the attack. Again, Herman's response to the situation was impressive: he took 73 wickets at 19.53. As in 1973 he played in every Championship game. He took 6 for 37 and 3 for 26 in the innings win over Sussex and in the next game took 5 for 58 *v.* Surrey.

Towards the end of the season, at Southampton, Hampshire had Glamorgan on the run; following on 237 behind, the visitors were reeling at 64 for 8 but held on for a draw that cost Hampshire the title: Herman finished with 6 for 15.

In 1975, however, it all started to go wrong: Roberts was missing for some of the time and Herman's comrade-in-arms in 1973, Tom Mottram, hardly played. Herman's mastery of line and length deserted him. He took fewer than 40 first-class wickets and in 1976, he dropped out altogether. It was a sad end to a career of genuine achievement.

# Colonel Christopher Heseltine

RHB, RF, 1895-1904

**Born:** 26 November 1869, London
**Died:** 13 June 1944, Walhampton, Lymington, Hants

**Batting**

| M | I | NO | Runs | Av |
|---|---|----|------|-----|
| 52 | 81 | 5 | 1039 | 13.67 |
| 50 | 100 | ct/st | | |
| 2 | - | 28 | | |

**Bowling**

| O | M | Runs | Wkts | Av |
|---|---|------|------|-----|
| 995 | 249 | 3185 | 116 | 27.45 |
| 5wl | 10wM | | | |
| 5 | - | | | |

**Best Performances**
77 *v.* Somerset, Portsmouth, 1899
7/106 *v.* Derbyshire, Derby, 1899

Over half-a-dozen seasons, Christopher Heseltine crammed in enough cricket for a lifetime, touring in India in 1892/93, South Africa in 1895/96 and the West Indies in 1896/97, as well as helping Hampshire when they regained first-class status in 1895. He had failed to obtain a place in the Eton eleven, and was no more successful at Cambridge, but was awarded a soccer blue in 1891. He had first played for Hampshire in their second-class days. Very tall, he took a long run and, arms flailing like a windmill, delivered the ball with a high action, putting, as C.B. Fry said of him, 'all the pace he knows into his deliveries.' Fry added that, 'on any fast ground he is liable to get wickets by sheer pace.' The great Surrey opening bat, Bobby Abel, had reason to confirm Fry's comments, as he fell to Heseltine, for a duck in three successive innings. In 1897, his best season, his victims numbered 41 at only 17.29 runs each including nine wickets for 61 runs against Surrey at Southampton. He was normally at his best for only a few overs, but in 1899 he mustered the energy to collect 7 wickets for 106 runs in an innings at Derby. He was not the bowler to prop up an increasingly ineffective attack, and service in the Boer War of 1899 to 1902 really brought an end to his playing career. In the 1914-18 war, although forty-five years of age, he rejoined the colours and serving with the Royal Fusiliers was twice mentioned in despatches. He remained, to the end of his life, a great supporter of the county, serving on the committee for many years. As president of the club from 1938 to 1944 he sustained its existence during the lean years of the Second World War.

# Arthur James Ledger Hill
RHB, RFM/ Lobs, 1895-1921

**Born:** 26 July 1871, Bassett, Southampton
**Died:** 6 September 1950, Spursholt, Romsey

**Batting**

| M | I | NO | Runs | Av |
|---|---|----|------|-----|
| 161 | 291 | 17 | 8381 | 30.58 |
| **50** | **100** | **ct/st** | | |
| 38 | 17 | 109 | | |

**Bowling**

| O | M | Runs | Wkts | Av |
|---|---|------|------|-----|
| 1993.4 | 465 | 6213 | 199 | 31.22 |
| **5wI** | **10wM** | | | |
| 3 | 1 | | | |

**Best Performances**
199 v. Surrey, The Oval, 1898
7/36 v. Leicestershire, Southampton, 1897

Arthur Hill was born in Bassett, north of Southampton, and made an early impact as a cricketer at Marlborough and Cambridge with free stroke play and fast-medium bowling, later turning to lobs. With these attributes, he helped Hampshire's advance to first-class status by many fine performances in 1894, when he scored 781 at an average of 41. He was for 15 years an invaluable member of the side, always welcome when he had time to spare from his numerous business interests. He toured South Africa with Lord Hawke's team in 1895/96, when he scored a century in the third of what have subsequently come to be regarded as test matches. He also toured in India, USA, and in 1911/12 in Argentina. His highest score came in 1899 when, in difficult circumstances, he hit 199 against Surrey. In 1905, he hit a century in each innings v. Somerset at Taunton: 124 and 118 not out. That season was his best, yielding 698 runs at an average of 46. He fared almost as well in 1899 and 1904, both seasons in which he excelled despite the county's general weaknesses, but through the demands of business he never played regularly enough to make a thousand runs in a season. C.B. Fry, who from 1909 was a colleague of Hill in the Hampshire team, had earlier written of him, 'When in form he is a batsman of the highest class; his best performances are usually done against strong bowling or on difficult wickets. He has plenty of stokes, in all of which he exhibits a striking knack of timing the ball – a characteristic that is the secret of his run getting. Perhaps his best strokes are on the off side. Some of his best off-drives pass close to point … He is able to play either very carefully or very freely, as the occasion requires.'

After 1908, as the side's progress went from strength to strength, he played less and less, but he retained his ability to pick up his bat and score runs which could be seen when he returned in 1919, and in his second match hit up 90 against Middlesex at Southampton.

In 1920, he and his son, A.E.L. Hill, both played for Hampshire, though not in the same match, and his last appearance came in the following year. For many years, before and after that, he served on the committee, of which he was chairman from 1935 to 1939.

# Gerry Hill

RHB, ROB, 1932-1954

**Born:** 15 April 1913, Totten, Hants

**Batting**

| M | I | NO | Runs | Av |
|---|---|----|------|-----|
| 371 | 595 | 94 | 9085 | 18.13 |
| **50** | **100** | ct/st | | |
| 28 | 4 | 169 | | |

**Bowling**

| O | M | Runs | Wkts | Av |
|---|---|------|------|-----|
| 7394 | 1797 | 18464 | 617 | 29.92 |
| **5wI** | **10wM** | | | |
| 18 | 3 | | | |

**Best Performances**

161 v. Sussex, Portsmouth, 1937
8/62 v. Kent, Tonbridge, 1935

Gerry Hill, from the New Forest was discovered by Sir Arthur Conan Doyle – himself a first-class cricketer – who recommended Hill to Hampshire. He joined the County as Jack Newman was leaving it, but he played with Mead, Brown, Kennedy and Boyes under the captaincy of Lionel Tennyson. By his last year on the staff (1954), he had also played with ten of the men who would bring the Championship to Hampshire for the first time.

Gerry made enough of an impression to be chosen for the County side in 1932. When Jim Bailey went off to League cricket, Kennedy became coach at Cheltenham College and a significant opportunity arose for a young bowler. Gerry Hill seized it eagerly, dismissing 93 victims in 1935 as well as scoring 549 runs, while two performances took him into the record books. At Tonbridge he took 8-62 against Kent and his match analysis of 14-146 was, at the time, the fourth best in the club's history. At the end of the match, he was awarded his cap.

His other record may seem less welcome, but it is a measure of the man that he has always found it hugely amusing. At Cardiff, Cyril Smart of Glamorgan hit him for 6, 6, 4, 6, 6, 4 – moving from 70* to his century in what was, then, the most expensive six-ball over in first-class cricket. Hill was less successful in 1936, although he took 5-14 v. Middlesex at Bournemouth, but came back with 80 wickets the following year, as well as enjoying his best season as a batsman which included his career best score of 161 v. Sussex at Portsmouth. There, he and 'Hooky' Walker put on 235, which is still Hampshire's fifth wicket record. He also took 6-89 and 7-71 in a narrow defeat by 21 runs at Birmingham.

In 1938, Gerry suffered a finger injury and, while he managed 823 runs and 33 wickets in 1938, he did not play during August or September.

War commenced with Gerry aged twenty-six. He was stationed in North Africa. After the war he returned to Hampshire, scoring 1,000 runs for the first time in 1946 and repeating the feat the following year. He also took around 50 wickets in each of those two years.

In 1948, Jim Bailey did the double and Charlie Knott took 89 wickets while Gerry was injured for some part of the season. He never retrieved his position as a leading bowler, although he took 12 wickets v. the Combined Services that year and continued to make useful runs including a sixth-wicket partnership of 202 with Jimmy Gray, v. Essex in 1952.

In 1954, he played few matches and his last appearance was at Guildford at the end of June against the great Surrey side of the 1950s. Hampshire were dismissed for 97, Surrey replied with 206-2 before declaring (May 117*) and Hampshire were hustled out for just 59. Gerry made a 'duck' in the first innings but top-scored in his final innings for the county, albeit with just 15.

Gerry had been one of five joint beneficiaries in the 1940s and had established a little business. He umpired quite a bit for the Second XI. He still lives in his native New Forest and, approaching ninety, continues to attend the reunions of former Hampshire players.

# Arthur Holt

RHB, Coach, 1935-1948

**Born:** 8 April 1911, Southampton
**Died:** 28 July 1994, Southampton

## Batting

| M | I | NO | Runs | Av |
|---|---|----|------|-----|
| 79 | 140 | 13 | 2853 | 22.46 |
| **50** | **100** | ct/st | | |
| 11 | 2 | 32 | | |

## Bowling

| O | M | Runs | Wkts | Av |
|---|---|------|------|-----|
| 5.4 | 0 | 47 | 1 | 47.00 |
| **5wI** | **10wM** | | | |
| - | - | | | |

## Best Performances

116 *v.* Leicestershire, Leicester, 1938
1/24 *v.* Warwickshire, Birmingham, 1939

Ask any Hampshire cricketer of the 1950s and 1960s about Arthur Holt and you can expect a response that mixes the brightest smiles with watery eyes. For two decades 'Holt's Colts' worked and played with a coach who had a vital role in the creation of Hampshire's first championship-winning side. Since he also discovered Gordon Greenidge and developed Jesty, Turner and Lewis, he was also a key figure in the second title-winners of 1973.

But Arthur Holt was not simply a coach. Southampton-born, he played soccer for his home-town team and after some good innings for the Deanery club he joined Hampshire in 1934 and made his first-class debut the following year. Although never a regular, he made centuries at Leicester in 1938 and Edgbaston in 1939, but like so many young men then lost the years of his cricketing maturity to the war.

In 1946 Arthur top-scored with 94, as Hampshire won their third match *v.* Essex at Portsmouth, and he finished the season in fourth place, with an average of 25. In the following seasons, he struggled to establish himself in a Hampshire side which combined the experience of Arnold, Bailey and McCorkell with the promise of Rogers. Gilbert Dawson was added in 1947 and Jimmy Gray in 1948 and with a place needed for the captain, Arthur's first-class career came to an end.

It was then that Desmond Eagar and the committee made the matchless decision to appoint Arthur as coach. In the 1950s this involved him principally in looking after the younger cricketers and in his first few years he worked closely with Sainsbury, Heath, Burden, Barnard and later Livingstone, Wassell, White, Bernard Harrison and Timms. He also persuaded the Saints defender Henry Horton to resume his cricket career and these ten cricketers with six others, won that first Championship in 1961. By then Arthur was working with the next generation including Bob Cottam and Alan Castell but he is remembered just as fondly by players like Peter Haslop and Tony Whibley who never managed to establish a career in the game. Whibley took what he had learned to his years as a teacher and cricket master at Lord Wandsworth College while Haslop, forty years after his one first-class appearance, was still coaching at Burridge. For that club he produced a coaching document which quoted Arthur, 'A good coach will learn that it is not always a case of what to tell the player but to have the courage to leave well alone – if it works, why change it?'

Arthur Holt died in the summer of 1994, but in such ways the legacy of this fundamentally good and kind man survives him.

**Born:** 18 April 1923, Colwall, Herefordshire
**Died:** 2 November 1998, Colwall

### Batting

| M | I | NO | Runs | Av |
|---|---|---|---|---|
| 405 | 723 | 80 | 21536 | 33.49 |
| **50** | **100** | ct/st | | |
| 122 | 32 | 254 | | |

### Bowling

| O | M | Runs | Wkts | Av |
|---|---|---|---|---|
| 51 | 15 | 162 | 3 | 54.00 |
| **5wl** | **10wM** | | | |
| - | - | | | |

### Best Performances

160* v. Yorkshire, Scarborough, 1961
2/0 v. Essex, Bournemouth, 1960

The most striking, but not the most significant, aspect of Henry Horton's batting was his stance, one of the unmistakable sights of county cricket at the time. Many writers tried to describe it but none did so better than A.A. Thomson. 'At the wicket [Horton] takes up what the lawyers would call an *a posteriori* position, not unlike that of a diver half-way through a jack-knife.'

Whatever the idiosyncrasies of his style, Horton, 'H', served Hampshire with distinction and gave an air of gravitas to proceedings frequently enlivened by the approach of the cavalier Roy Marshall. Some have taken the view that the immensely reliable Horton was a more influential figure in a fourth innings run-chase than the great West Indian. Marshall himself said that Horton was the sort of player you would want in your side if your life depended on it.

He came to Hampshire relatively late in life. He played a few games for his native Worcestershire but football was his first calling and he had a successful career as a half-back for Blackburn Rovers, being transferred to Southampton for £10,000 (a club record for Blackburn at the time) in 1951. At Southampton he met Arthur Holt, the County's coach. One thing led to another and he made his debut in 1953. By 1955, he was a regular in the team and was awarded his county cap.

Courage, discipline and dependability were the qualities most closely associated with Horton's batting. Physical courage was exemplified by his taking the field for Southampton with a broken jaw. He played very straight and was a strong driver, although he was usually content with what Arlott described as a 'short deliberate push' which could find gaps in the field with just enough force to cross the boundary. When suitably roused, he could hit as hard as anyone. In 1959 he scored 2,478 runs at 47.60 with 4 hundreds and 16 fifties. He scored over 2,000 runs in 1960 (7 centuries and 10 fifties) and 1961 (4 centuries and 17 fifties) and only failed by 23 runs to do so in 1962.

As he got older – and he was forty-four in his last year (1967) – he got slower. Against Leicestershire at Coalville in 1966, Horton displayed what *Wisden* described, tactfully, as 'monumental patience' in compiling 147 not out in seven and a half hours. Hampshire's scoring rate was a fraction under two an over.

After retirement, Horton served on the first-class umpires' list and also coached for a while at Worcestershire and at the Royal Grammar School, Worcester before returning to his birthplace, Colwall, where he died in 1998.

# Colin Ingleby-MacKenzie
## LHB, WKT, 1951-1965

**Born:** 15 September 1933, Dartmouth, Devon

**Batting**

| M | I | NO | Runs | Av |
|---|---|----|------|-----|
| 309 | 513 | 60 | 11140 | 24.59 |

| 50 | 100 | ct/st | | |
|----|-----|-------|---|---|
| 49 | 10 | 186 | | |

**Bowling**

| O | M | Runs | Wkts | Av |
|---|---|------|------|-----|
| 6.4 | 1 | 22 | 0 | - |

| 5wI | 10wM |
|-----|------|
| - | - |

**Best Performances**
132* v. Essex, Cowes (IOW), 1961

As the first Hampshire captain to lead his side to a Championship title, Colin Ingleby-Mackenzie is assured of a place in the County's folklore. The success of the 1961 champions, universally popular (except in the broad and somewhat grudging acres of Yorkshire, where, thirty years later, former players were still claiming that they 'was robbed') was based on the hard work of a number of people – Desmond Eagar and Arthur Holt among them. But the debonair and engaging old Etonian 'Ingleby' made a vital contribution with what *Wisden* called his 'hitherto unknown talent for master strategy.'

At the centre of the Yorkshire gripe was the perception that opponents were more likely to be generous to Hampshire in setting a target than they were to their northern rivals. The fact is, that although out of Hampshire's 19 wins (out of 32 matches: Yorkshire won 17) 10 came as a result of Hampshire declaring in their third innings and setting a target, timing was everything. Whether it was a first (there was no follow-on that year in the Championship) or second innings declaration, Ingleby-Mackenzie had a gambler's instinct for choosing the right moment. In a celebrated game against Gloucestershire, who had been bowled out for 176 with the second day lost to rain, Ingleby-Mackenzie declared Hampshire's first innings at 96 for no wicket. It was not a universally popular decision –

when Roy Marshall eventually made his way back to the dressing room he threw his bat at the skipper – but it was triumphantly vindicated. Set 196 to win at 88 an hour, Hampshire got home by two wickets with three minutes to spare. Furthermore, it somehow set the tone for the season. Arthur Milton, captaining Gloucestershire, had been prepared to keep the game alive and Ingleby-Mackenzie found that other opposing captains took the same approach.

Ingleby-Mackenzie's subsequent success in the city suggests that there was more to his captaincy than a fondness for a flutter and an insistence that his players were back in the hotel in time for breakfast. The key lay, to a large extent, in man-management. Ingleby-Mackenzie was one of the youngest men in the side, yet he was able to weld some forceful characters together. Significantly, his closest personal bond was with the oldest member, the humorous and worldly wicketkeeper Leo Harrison, a pre-war veteran for whom Ingleby capably deputised behind the stumps from time to time.

Certainly no one could have accused him of being obsessed with his role or with the game. 'I see Leicester had a good day yesterday, skipper', said Henry Horton over a break-

fast newspaper. 'Ah yes,' replied his insouciant leader, 'he's a good jockey that fellow.'

Like all successful captains he was lucky. In early May, Hampshire beat Surrey by five wickets having been outplayed for two days. Surrey lost only six wickets in the match but Marshall destroyed their attack in the fourth innings. Wisden commended Surrey's enterprise, compared with Hampshire's 'negative tactics' over the first two days.

As a batsman, his most important contribution in that memorable year was against Essex in the last game the County played at Cowes. Coming in at 35 for 4 with Hampshire still needing 206 to win and with Marshall injured he made what *Wisden* called a 'brilliant' 132 in less than two and a half hours. A powerful left-hander, he was at his best on the attack, relying largely on one shot, elegantly described by Marshall as 'a cross-batted swipe'. He won the prize for scoring the fastest hundred of the season in 1958: 100 in 61 minutes *v*. Somerset at Bournemouth; he was already the front runner in that particular competition for his hundred against Kent, and in an early example of master strategy he had paid £25 to insure the £100 prize, thus effectively winning the prize money twice minus the premium.

Although Hampshire rose from twelfth to first in 1961, their success was not wholly unexpected. Ingleby-Mackenzie, who first played for the county in 1951, had been handpicked for the captaincy by Eagar. They were effectively joint captains in 1957. In 1958, Ingleby-Mackenzie's first full year in charge (he was twenty-four and was voted Best Young Cricketer of the Year, the only serving captain to have won that accolade), Hampshire came second to Surrey. After 1961, however, the sparkle, or the genie, appeared to have departed from the bottle. Ingleby still had one surprise declaration up his sleeve, however. In 1965, in one of his last games in charge, an apparently rain-ruined affair *v*. Worcestershire, he declared Hampshire's first innings closed 146 behind Worcestershire, who in effect forfeited their second innings and bowled Hampshire out for 31 securing the Championship and bringing the premature celebrations of Northamptonshire to a sorry end. *Wisden* tut-tutted, deploring the incidence of 'manufactured finishes' in County matches.

Ingleby-Mackenzie was an outstanding president of MCC, paving the way for the admission of women as members. He is currently the president of Hampshire.

# Kevan James
LHB, LFM, 1985-1999

**Born:** 18 March 1961, Lambeth

## Batting

| M | I | NO | Runs | Av |
|---|---|---|---|---|
| 204 | 315 | 51 | 8189 | 31.01 |
| 50 | 100 | ct/st | | |
| 42 | 10 | 75 | | |

## Bowling

| O | M | Runs | Wkts | Av |
|---|---|---|---|---|
| 3757.3 | 833 | 11657 | 359 | 32.47 |
| 5wI | 10wM | | | |
| 10 | 1 | | | |

## Best Performances
162 v. Glamorgan, Cardiff, 1989
8/49 v. Somerset, Basingstoke, 1989

Kevan James' career figures suggest that he was a workaday player, muddling through county cricket as a 'bits and pieces' performer. That, however, would be a harsh judgment. Although James constantly flirted with the humdrum throughout his fifteen years with Hampshire, he was an enthusiast who sporadically produced quite startling performances.

James was a genuine left-handed all-rounder – a relatively rare breed. He was a left-handed batsman usually of the dogged rather than the debonair variety and a canny, nagging bowler of left-arm medium-paced swing. Of average ability, he made himself into a cricketer capable of exceptional deeds.

Within weeks of joining Hampshire in 1985, after five years with Middlesex, James batted himself into the County's record books, putting on 227 for the eighth wicket v. Somerset with Tim Tremlett – James' share was 124. A month later, the Australians were routed for 76 at Southampton and James, who up to that point had taken two first-class wickets in his career, opened the bowling with Cardigan Connor and took 6 for 22.

In 1987, he scored 620 runs in 10 completed innings with 2 hundreds including a belligerent 142 v. Nottinghamshire with 3 sixes and 20 fours. He finished top of Hampshire's batting averages and was the third-highest placed Englishman in the national averages. In 1997, he topped Hampshire's bowling averages (as he had done in 1988 and 1993) and was fourth – the second Englishman – in the national averages. This was largely attributable to a remarkable performance v. Somerset at Basingstoke. Needing 235 to win, Somerset reached 175 for 3 but the thirty-six-year-old James took 8 for 49 to win the match for Hampshire by 9 runs and earn match figures of 13 for 94.

As a batsman, he occupied most positions in the order from one to nine at some point. (Indeed, when playing for Wellington in New Zealand they put him in at number 10 or 11.) His best season with the bat was 1991 when he scored 1,274 runs at an average of 47.18 (as well as taking 41 wickets). In 1990, injury restricted him to one match – the first of the season v. Kent at Canterbury where he scored 50 and 104 not out.

But these achievements pale into insignificance compared with James' performance v. the Indians at Southampton in July 1996. The tourists, batting first, were coasting at 207 for 1 when James suddenly dismissed Jadeja, Tendulkar, Dravid and Manjrekar – not a bad haul in 4 balls. That was astonishing enough, but James was not finished yet. When Hampshire batted, he scored a hundred batting at number 4. Today, and probably for all time, in *Wisden*, under the heading 'Hundred and Four Wickets with Consecutive Balls', there is just one name: K.D. James.

# Arthur Jaques
RFM, RHB, 1913-1914

**Born:** 7 March 1888, Shanghai, China
**Died:** 27 September 1915, Bois, Hugo, Loos, France

## Batting

| M | I | NO | Runs | Av |
|---|---|----|------|-----|
| 49 | 80 | 16 | 864 | 13.50 |
| 50 | 100 | ct/st | | |
| 1 | - | 29 | | |

## Bowling

| O | M | Runs | Wkts | Av |
|---|---|------|------|-----|
| 1454.1 | 361 | 3617 | 168 | 21.52 |
| 5wI | 10wM | | | |
| 10 | 3 | | | |

**Best Performances**
68 v. Worcestershire, Southampton, 1914
8/21 v. Somerset, Bath, 1914

This lanky, medium-paced bowler played only two seasons for the County. In 1913, his performances were unremarkable, but the following year they were something different and his method of attack earned much attention. From a longish run, he delivered the ball from a great height; relying on the in-swinger as his stock ball, which he pitched on the wicket or outside the leg stump, with a crowd of fieldsmen close in on the leg side. He also imparted a sharp off-break and so cramped the batsman that sooner or later he exhausted their patience. He dismissed 14 Derbyshire batsmen for 105 at Basingstoke, took 7 for 51 in the second innings of Warwickshire at Southampton, and had a big hand in the victory over Kent at Bournemouth at the beginning of September, with nine victims for 86. At Bath in June, he and Alec Kennedy bowled unchanged to dismiss Somerset for 83 and 38 and give Hampshire victory by an innings and 192 runs. Jaques' tally was 14 wickets for 54. He played for the Gentlemen v. the Players at the Oval and Lord's, but his tactics did not impress and he took only two wickets, bowling only three overs at Lord's.

Earlier, he was a member of the eleven at Aldenham School, where in 1907 he took 43 wickets at under 11 runs per wicket. He went on to Cambridge, where he played in the Freshman's match in 1908, taking 3 wickets

for 29 and 1 for 15, which suggests that he might have been given a further trial. His best cricket had been played for Hampshire Hogs, before he toured the West Indies with MCC. He took only five wickets in the Caribbean, but a trial with Hampshire in 1913 followed and he captured 53 wickets which cost over 28 runs each. Over three seasons, he failed to find a place in the Cambridge University side.

His death in the First World War limited his career to those two seasons. His moderate performance for the Gentlemen gave rise to the thought that top-class opponents might have found ways of defeating his methods in the course of two or three further seasons, but he may just have been nervous on the great occasion at Lord's or for some other reason been below his best. How his career may have developed is impossible to tell, but it was widely anticipated that he would ultimately succeed Sprot in the captaincy. Shortly before his death he was married, but in the will that he made on that occasion he remembered the county club by leaving it a legacy of £500.

# Trevor Jesty
RHB, RFM, 1966-1984

**Born:** 2 June 1948, Gosport, Hants

## Batting

| M | I | NO | Runs | Av |
|---|---|---|---|---|
| 340 | 538 | 74 | 14753 | 31.79 |
| **50** | **100** | **ct/st** | | |
| 70 | 26 | 200/1 | | |

## Bowling

| O | M | Runs | Wkts | Av |
|---|---|---|---|---|
| 5216.3 | 1375 | 13596 | 475 | 28.62 |
| **5wI** | **10wM** | | | |
| 14 | - | | | |

## Best Performances
248 v. Cambridge University, Cambridge, 1984
7/75 v. Worcestershire, Southampton, 1976

As a right-handed stroke-player, Gosport-born Trevor Jesty lost little in comparison with Barry Richards in terms of style. Fair-haired like Richards, but of medium height and stocky in build, his sumptuous off-side shots were a special joy and in the 1980s he was one of the most attractive batsmen in the country as well as being a reliable run-scorer. Given that he was a more than useful medium-pace bowler and a good fielder, his failure to win Test recognition is one of the great unsolved mysteries of English cricket.

Jesty made his debut in 1966 and earned a regular place in the side in 1969 as much on the basis of promise and all-round utility as of genuine achievement – in those days he was effectively a bowler who could bat rather than the batsman who could bowl of later years.

Thus, in the 1973 Championship-winning season he took 35 wickets at 20.54 in only 276 overs but had a modest return with the bat. In 1975, when he was already being talked of as a potential England player, he came second to Roberts in the County's bowling averages, capturing 50 wickets at 19. But 1976, a poor year for the team, was at last a breakthrough year for Jesty with the bat as he easily passed a thousand runs for the first time and scored his maiden hundred, v. Gloucestershire. He also followed it up with

159 not out v. Somerset, out of a total of 296 – Ian Botham had reduced Hampshire from 47 for 1 to 52 for 6.

Jesty's *annus mirabilis* was 1982. He had had a poor year with the bat in 1981 – although he took 52 wickets at 19.86 – but in 1982 everything clicked. He scored 1,645 runs at 58.75 with 8 centuries – only Philip Mead (three times) has scored more centuries in a season for Hampshire. As Jesty also took 35 wickets at 21, an England call-up seemed a reasonable hope but it was not to be. Jesty flew out to Australia as a reinforcement that winter and played in 10 one-day internationals. He was in England's World Cup squad in 1983 but did not play.

He played some memorable one-day innings for Hampshire, in particular, in the Sunday League. He scored 96 in 40 minutes against Somerset in 1980, with 6 sixes and 11 fours, and 166 not out v. Surrey in 1983 sharing an unbroken stand of 269 for the second wicket with Gordon Greenidge. His tidy swing howling made him a formidable performer in one-day cricket – in that same game v. Surrey, Jesty became the first player to score 4,000 runs and take 200 wickets in the Sunday League. Only Cardigan Connor has taken more Sunday League wickets for Hampshire than Jesty.

As vice-captain he deputised frequently for Nick Pocock until, twenty minutes before the start of play against Warwickshire in July 1984, it was announced that Mark Nicholas would lead the side for the rest of the season. Jesty joined Surrey for 1985. He subsequently played for Lancashire and is now a first-class umpire.

# Neil Johnson

LHB, RM, 2001-2002

**Born:** 24 January 1970, Harare, Zimbabwe

### Batting

| M | I | NO | Runs | Av |
|---|---|----|------|-----|
| 34 | 56 | 5 | 1930 | 37.84 |
| 50 | 100 | ct/st | | |
| 14 | 3 | 55 | | |

### Bowling

| O | M | Runs | Wkts | Av |
|---|---|------|------|-----|
| 495.1 | 94 | 1725 | 45 | 38.33 |
| 5wI | 10wM | | | |
| - | - | | | |

### Best Performances

117 v. Kent, Canterbury, 2002,
4/20 v. Derbyshire, Rose Bowl, 2001

Whoever was to take on the role of Hampshire's overseas player in 2002 was going to have a daunting task. First, that player would have to step into the shoes of Shane Warne. Secondly, and in a sense paradoxically, he would have to make up for the disappointments of 2000 and help the County get back into Division One of the County Championship.

The choice of Zimbabwe-born Neil Johnson proved a shrewd one. On paper, Johnson was an excellent candidate as an overseas player. He had proved himself at international level – he was one of the individual successes of the 1999 World Cup in England and had a good record, particularly as a batsman, for Leicestershire in 1997 and over a number of years for Natal. What made him even better was that he had now retired from international cricket so there was no danger of his suddenly being whisked away to play in Sharjah for a fortnight in the middle of June. He was ideal and if he could have produced a Portuguese grandparent he would have been perfect.

Johnson turned out to be as valuable an acquisition as his record suggested. Given the frailty of Hampshire's top order in 2000, and the gap in terms of wickets brought about by Warne's departure, it was difficult to determine whether he was needed more desperately for his solid but enterprising left-handed batting or his fast-medium right-arm bowling. In the event, he turned out to be a valuable contributor with both, as well as a reliable slip fielder.

Johnson was the only Hampshire batsman to reach a thousand runs in first-class cricket at an average of 44.70. Batting turned out to be his stronger suit. His 23 first-class wickets cost 39.60 apiece. Only David Byas of Yorkshire took more than Johnson's 28 catches.

After a slow start, he was scoring very steadily in May and June, hitting five half-centuries in six innings. He finished the season with 2 centuries in three matches. At Worcester he took the first 3 wickets to fall in the match and then scored 103, with 14 fours and 3 sixes in conditions which most of the batsmen of both sides found trying. Against Nottinghamshire at Trent Bridge he scored 105 not out, helping Hampshire get the bonus points they needed to finish runners-up in Division Two. As Johnson was also the county's leading run-scorer in the National League, his value to the side cannot be disputed.

Unfortunately, a strong start and a reasonable finish could not disguise a disappointing 2002. Although Johnson was Hampshire's leading run-scorer in the Championship, more had been expected from a player of his ability and dedication.

# Colonel A.C. Johnston

RHB, RM, 1902-1919

**Born:** 26 January 1884, Derby
**Died:** 27 December 1952, Knaphill, Woking, Surrey

**Batting**

| M | I | NO | Runs | Av |
|---|---|----|------|-----|
| 108 | 190 | 13 | 5442 | 30.74 |
| 50 | 100 | ct/st | | |
| 27 | 10 | 57/1 | | |

**Bowling**

| O | M | Runs | Wkts | Av |
|---|---|------|------|-----|
| 151.4 | 8 | 805 | 18 | 44.72 |
| 5wI | 10wM | | | |
| - | - | | | |

**Best Performances**
175 *v.* Warwickshire, Coventry, 1912
4/21 *v.* Somerset, Bournemouth, 1904

Alec Johnston came to the County side by way of the Winchester College eleven. The family's connection with the County arose from his father's position as Director General of the Ordnance Survey, then a military post at Southampton. Sir Duncan Johnston had himself played four times for Derbyshire in 1882. Of all the Army batsmen who played for Hampshire in the twentieth century, he has claims to be the greatest, always triumphantly surmounting the long gaps between his appearances. He hit his first hundreds (two) in County cricket in 1904, aged twenty and went on to head the Hampshire averages two years later, when his figures were 39.26 for 903 runs, and he repeated the feat in 1910, when his total was 1,158 runs at 36.18 an innings.

Johnston surpassed these achievements in 1912 (one of the wettest seasons on record and so a year of low scoring) when in 20 innings, once not out, he totalled 1,044 runs, and averaged 54.94, including 3 centuries among them. He scored 175 *v.* Warwickshire at Coventry, which was his highest first-class innings, and followed it with an undefeated century in the second innings. Of greater class still was his performance for the Gentlemen at Lord's, bearing in mind the importance of the occasion and the quality of the attack, which included Barnes, Hitch, Dean, Hearne and

Albert Relf. In the Gentlemen's first innings, he top-scored on a difficult pitch with 89. In first and out eighth at 222, he was the only member of the side to score more than 37. He came very close to selection for England in the Triangular Tournament against Australia and South Africa, but legend has it that he could not be contacted by Fry, the England captain – their paths had crossed when each was on a different platform at Southampton station at the same time! That season, three Hampshire batsmen headed the first-class batting averages, C.B. Fry, A.C. Johnston and Phil Mead.

A very determined character, regarded by some as a difficult man, he excelled with drives on both sides of the wicket, and powerful hits to leg. He needed all his reserves and stubbornness after the fracture of a femur in the First World War left his right leg over four inches shorter than his left. He appeared once only and with success in 1919, but the reluctance of the authorities, led by Lord Harris, to permit the war-wounded to have the use of a runner brought his first-class career to an end. He continued for many years to play in regimental and club cricket with the aid of a runner, conserving his energy and batting for long scores, so troubling the scorers and bowlers and confusing many a fielding side.

# Will Kendall

RHB, RM, 1996 to date

**Born:** 18 December 1973, Wimbledon

### Batting

| M | I | NO | Runs | Av |
|---|---|----|------|-----|
| 99 | 170 | 17 | 5039 | 32.93 |
| 50 | 100 | ct/st | | |
| 26 | 6 | 90 | | |

### Bowling

| O | M | Runs | Wkts | Av |
|---|---|------|------|-----|
| 108.3 | 17 | 349 | 5 | 69.8 |
| 5wI | 10wM | | | |
| - | - | | | |

### Best Performances

201* v. Sussex, Southampton, 1999
2/46 v. Nottinghamshire, Southampton, 1996

Will Kendall, an Oxford blue who scored 145 not out in the 1996 University match, has the talent and the determination to be a leading figure in Hampshire cricket over the next decade. Like most of Hampshire's batsmen, however, he has struggled in the last couple of years. Indeed, by the end of 2002 Kendall had reached fifty only twice in first-class cricket at the Rose Bowl, both in losing causes in 2002 (he carried his bat in the second innings against Leicestershire). There is no doubt, however, that he has the ability and the hunger to find form again.

In 2000, he was comfortably Hampshire's leading batsman, scoring over 1,100 runs at an average of 41, with three centuries when nobody else made 800 runs. Two of the hundreds came in successive victories over Durham and Derbyshire and there was only one other win for the County that summer.

At his best, a fluent and attractive stroke-player, Kendall's greatest assets are his composure and patience which enable him to play the long innings so essential in four-day cricket. This was best exemplified in his match-saving second-innings double century against Sussex in 1999 (when he was also the

county's leading run-scorer) in which he faced 404 balls and hit 32 fours, receiving his cap at the end of it. This must also have prompted the decision to promote him to open in 2002 although it is not clear whether that is the best position for him. In one-day cricket he tends to bat down the order, scoring useful runs and, less predictably, taking useful wickets with his apparently innocuous medium pace.

Will Kendall is a well-rounded character (he writes an entertaining review of the season for *The Hampshire Handbook*) and a good, all-round sportsman – for example, he is a useful enough soccer player to have been offered terms by Reading. With his Bradfield and Oxford credentials, seasoned observers of Hampshire cricket had Kendall marked down as a future captain almost from the moment he arrived in the second half of the 1996 season. Appointed vice-captain to Robin Smith in 2001, his first prolonged spell as stand-in leader came at a time in 2002 when collective and individual confidence seemed to be draining away. One thing is for sure, Hampshire's probable future captain is a man of principle to whom cricket's increasingly derided values actually mean something. The next couple of years, playing under Shane Warne, will be especially challenging for Kendall.

# Alexander S. Kennedy
RFM, RHB, 1907-1936

**Born:** 24 January 1891, Edinburgh
**Died:** 15 November 1959, Hythe,
    Southampton

**Batting**

| M | I | NO | Runs | Av |
|---|---|----|------|-----|
| 596 | 916 | 110 | 14925 | 18.51 |
| 50 | 100 | ct/st | | |
| 59 | 10 | 482 | | |

**Bowling**

| O | M | Runs | Wkts | Av |
|---|---|------|------|-----|
| 22359 | 6108 | 53950 | 2549 | 21.16 |
| 5wI | 10wM | | | |
| 205 | 41 | | | |

**Best Performances**
163* v. Warwickshire, Portsmouth, 1923
9/33 v. Lancashire, Liverpool, 1920

Alec Kennedy was the best kind of professional accepting that for every day of triumph (of which there were many) there would be dozens when fine weather, easy-paced wickets or dreamy fieldsmen made for very hard work indeed. John Arlott wrote one of his best pieces on the technique of cricket about the bowling of Kennedy on such a day, 'They could not on the merciless pitches of the 1920s and '30s hope to beat and bowl the great batsmen in a defensive stroke. Their aim was, by minute variations of pace and length, by strategy as fine as the checking of the ball by following through onto a bent leg, to deny the batsman the comfort of playing the ball in the middle of the bat. Sooner or later the batsman would make the infinitesimal error which is the difference between a stroke hit straight along the ground and the one which sends the ball the catchable inch off it.'

He hit his peak early in 1912, aged only twenty-one, when his victims numbered 139. Between then and 1932, he took over one hundred wickets in a season 13 times. After the First World War, his batting developed and he achieved the double four times, three years in succession from 1921 to 1923 and again in 1928. In 1922, his victims numbered over 200. He and his great partner, Jack Newman, twice bowled unchanged through

both innings of a match. He three times achieved the hat-trick. In 1921, he seized 8 Glamorgan wickets before lunch at Cardiff. The following season v. Somerset at Bath, his 15 wickets in the match cost only 116 runs. Eight years later, his analysis was 14 wickets for 87 at Swansea. In 1927, he returned figures of 7 wickets for 8 runs against the strong batting of Warwickshire at Portsmouth. The same year he caused a sensation by taking all ten wickets for Players v. Gentlemen at the Oval.

When selected to tour South Africa for MCC in 1922/23, he took full advantage of the opportunity, claiming 32 victims in the five tests, average 19.32, and followed with 21 wickets there the following winter in unofficial tests. Following a very long run, he bowled with a very high action and a flick of the wrist, which at one time led to suspicion that he threw the ball. He was never no-balled for throwing in 26 seasons of English cricket, but the selectors were wary and this great player never took part in a Test match at home. Yet, his County career was one of continuing success; as late as 1934, his last full season, he achieved 990 runs at an average of 24.14 and 91 wickets at 29.26 each, a fine performance by a man of forty-

Alec Kennedy and his wife on board the *Capetown Castle* on their arrival at Southampton in April 1954.

three, in a long hot summer. He owed much of his success to consistent length, pace (on the fast side of medium) and in-swing, coupled with off-spin from the pitch. At the end of 1934, he was appointed coach at Cheltenham College, but returned to Hampshire in the school holidays. They had changed the lbw law for that season on an experimental basis; the off-spinner turning in from outside the stumps and hitting the batsman's pads could now achieve a leg before wicket dismissal. In seven matches, Kennedy claimed 32 wickets!

After the Second World War, he went as a coach to South Africa, where he joined his old bowling partner, Jack Newman, and was followed by Neil McCorkell in 1951. He returned to Southampton in 1954, took up bowls and kept a newsagents and tobacconists until his death in 1959. Businesslike and prudent in all his activities, he took life very seriously. He was a good man to have on your side, match by match and season by season. Jack Newman wrote of him: 'No day was too long for Alec. Although we think of him as a great bowler, he was also a very sound batsman and could easily have kept his place as such. He also had one of the safest pairs of hands in cricket. One often hears the remark that so and so was unlucky not to play in Test matches, and one feels that this remark applied to dear old Alec.'

# C.J. 'Charlie' Knott
RHB, OB, 1938-1954

**Born:** 26 November 1914, Southampton

## Batting

| M | I | NO | Runs | Av |
|---|---|----|------|-----|
| 166 | 235 | 94 | 1003 | 7.11 |
| 50 | 100 | ct/st | | |
| - | - | 55 | | |

## Bowling

| O | M | Runs | Wkts | Av |
|---|---|------|------|-----|
| 5461.1 | 1213 | 15224 | 647 | 23.53 |
| 5wI | 10wM | | | |
| 44 | 8 | | | |

## Best Performances
27 v. Sussex, Worthing, 1951
8/26 v. Cambridge University, Bournemouth, 1951

'Every day was a lovely day, win lose or draw.'
(CJK)

John Arlott once described Charlie Knott as the finest amateur bowler to appear for Hampshire but he was more than that. Playing throughout his career in some of Hampshire's weakest sides, he was often their main bowler and he took his 647 wickets at almost four every match. This average has been bettered by just three of Hampshire's leading bowlers Shackleton, Kennedy and Andy Roberts. In addition, Knott's runs per wicket average of 23.53 is superior to Boyes, Newman and Sainsbury.

When Charlie was called into the Hampshire attack in 1938, he bowled medium pace and had just one wicket from two matches so, for the third game at Cheltenham, he turned to off-spin from the same ten pace run-up. Here he enjoyed more success with his first five-wicket haul including the young Gloucestershire amateur Desmond Eagar.

In the following year, he showed his progress with 8-85 v. Surrey at Portsmouth and was awarded his county cap by letter following the end of the season.

When cricket resumed, he was already thirty-one years old and he lost no time in establishing himself. He bowled magnificently against the Indian tourists, taking 7-36, took five or more wickets in an innings on 12 occasions, finished the season with 121 wickets and played in the Test Trial and for the Gentlemen v. Players at Lord's.

He was injured for much of 1947, but came back with 101 wickets in the Australian summer of 1948 and the same number in 1949. That season was the first in which Derek Shackleton took 100 wickets for the County, easing the burden on Charlie.

From 1946, Charlie was the vice-captain to his good friend Desmond Eagar and in 1950 he captained the side in five of their last six matches, including a remarkable win at Eastbourne. Sussex needed just 98 to win, but Charlie took 5-5 in seven overs and Hampshire won by 60 runs! During that year, he appeared for the Gentlemen again and was the last player to perform the hat-trick in that famous fixture. He was on the shortlist for the tour to Australia, but international honours never came.

In 1953 he recorded his best figures, 8-36, v. Nottinghamshire at Bournemouth, but business pressures became increasingly demanding and he retired in the following season just as Hampshire were introducing the young spinners Burden and Sainsbury.

Some of his greatest achievements came as cricket chairman in the 1970s and 1980s. In his new role they won a Championship, three Sunday League titles and their first Lord's final. The young man from Southampton who learned to bowl in the city's parks gave a lifetime to Hampshire cricket and still enjoys his visits to watch the team he loves.

**Born:** 19 October 1859, Wareham, Dorset
**Died:** 26 May 1946, Sutton Veny, Wiltshire

**Batting**

| M | I | NO | Runs | Av |
|---|---|----|------|-----|
| 33 | 59 | 8 | 2028 | 39.76 |

| 50 | 100 | ct/st | | |
|----|-----|-------|--|--|
| 10 | 4 | 26 | | |

**Bowling**

| O | M | Runs | Wkts | Av |
|---|---|------|------|-----|
| 311.1 | 153 | 942 | 45 | 20.93 |

| 5wI | 10wM | | | |
|-----|------|--|--|--|
| 3 | 1 | | | |

**Best Performances**
211 *v.* Kent, Southampton, 1884
7/149 *v.* Sussex, Hove, 1882

Educated at Sherborne School and Caius College, Cambridge, Lacey won blues for Association Football and cricket. He captained Hampshire from 1888 to 1893, when the County was not regarded as first class. His batting was one of the brighter features of that lean period, notably when he amassed 323 not out against Norfolk in 1887. Three years earlier he had excelled against Kent in a match which did have first-class status by scoring 211 and 92 not out. He played a little after the County entered the championship in 1895 and scored 121 *v.* Derbyshire at Southampton in 1897, but virtually withdrew from active play on his appointment in 1898, from a list of over 50 candidates, as secretary of MCC. A barrister by profession, he had, as Tony Lewis wrote, a meticulous concern for detail, and combined patient, hard work with a fine brain. His first task was to recover the financial situation of MCC. Some regarded him as a cold individual who never dropped his official guard, but over the next decade he reorganised the club, splitting it into separate departments run by sub-committees, started Easter coaching classes for members' sons, and saw the inauguration of the Board of Control for home Test matches in 1899. In 1903, MCC took over the organisation of England touring sides overseas and the establishment of the Advisory County Cricket Committee in 1904. To complete a decade or so of development, in 1909 came the formation of the Imperial (now International) Cricket Conference, which ultimately became the parliament of Test-playing countries.

Lacey continued in the post until 1926. He received a knighthood on his retirement – the first individual to receive the honour for services to cricket. He had suffered the loss of his wife and only child while quite a young man. He subsequently married the widow of a member of the Walker whisky distilling family. His stepson was Rob Walker, the motor racing entrepreneur, for whose team five World Champions drove in the 1950s and 1960s including Stirling Moss, John Cooper and Jack Brabham.

# Danny Livingstone
LHB, WKT, 1959-1972

**Born:** 21 September 1933, St John's, Antigua, West Indies
**Died:** 8 September 1988, Antigua

### Batting

| M | I | NO | Runs | Av |
|---|---|---|---|---|
| 299 | 516 | 63 | 12660 | 27.94 |
| 50 | 100 | ct/st | | |
| 65 | 16 | 240/2 | | |

### Bowling

| O | M | Runs | Wkts | Av |
|---|---|---|---|---|
| 18.2 | 6 | 68 | 1 | 68.00 |
| 5wl | 10wM | | | |
| - | - | | | |

### Best Performances
200 v. Surrey, Southampton, 1962
1/31 v. Surrey, The Oval, 1968

There are two things that every Hampshire supporter of the early 1960s remembers about Danny Livingstone, the Antiguan left-handed middle-order batsman.

The first is his catch (justly described as the most famous in Hampshire's history) to dismiss Bob Taylor of Derbyshire at Dean Park in September 1961, winning the match for Hampshire and thus ensuring that they won the Championship for the first time in their history.

The second is Livingstone's remarkable innings v. Surrey at Southampton at the end of the 1962 season. He came in on a hat-trick with Hampshire at 37 for 2 and was dropped first ball. Before long Hampshire were 128 for 8. Then Livingstone and Alan Castell put on 230, still the third highest ninth-wicket partnership in English cricket. Livingstone scored 200, his highest score, with 3 sixes and 22 fours.

When he came to Hampshire, he was a flamboyant strokeplayer – Roy Marshall marvelled at his natural talent. Livingstone transformed himself over the years into a disciplined and phlegmatic run-getter. Dapper and polished, he was always attractive to watch. He gave an early indication of his potential in a low-scoring game v. Middlesex at Lord's in 1960, when his 66 was the only score of over fifty in the game.

He established himself in 1961 scoring 1,643 runs including a maiden century against Northamptonshire. In 1963, his 151 against the West Indians was the highest score made against them. In 1964 he was the County's leading run-scorer with 1,671 runs at 35.55 including 4 centuries with two in the match v. Kent at Canterbury, making him the first Hampshire batsman to achieve the feat since Jack Newman in 1927.

The following year, however, he suffered a startling decline in form, scoring fewer than 700 runs at an average of 18 and losing his place. He fought his way back, putting on 272 for the third wicket with Henry Horton against Leicestershire in 1966, and in 1967 he reached a thousand runs. He was one of four batsmen to pass a thousand runs in 1970, putting on a record 263 for the fourth wicket v. Middlesex with Roy Marshall.

He took only one first-class wicket, but it was a distinguished if somewhat poignant one – Ken Barrington in his last game for Surrey in 1968.

'The quiet Antiguan', as John Arlott called him, every September disappeared into the anonymity of north London, before his return to Antigua, where he eventually became Director of Sport on the island. He died in 1989.

# Walter Livsey

RHB, WKT, 1913-1929

**Born:** 23 September 1893, Todmorden, Yorkshire

**Died:** 12 September 1978, Merton Park, London

## Batting

| M | I | NO | Runs | Av |
|---|---|---|---|---|
| 309 | 443 | 131 | 4818 | 15.44 |
| **50** | **100** | **ct/st** | | |
| 11 | 2 | 375/254 | | |

## Best Performance

110* v. Warwickshire, Birmingham, 1922

Walter Livsey was born in Todmorden, but was still a baby when the family moved to Surrey. He kept wicket from his schooldays, and played at the Oval in schoolboy games. Strudwick of Surrey was one of the great stumpers of the day, and Sullivan was his well-established deputy, so Livsey accepted an invitation to join Hampshire in 1912. Qualifying in 1914, he dismissed 62 batsmen that season, 39 caught and 23 stumped – a feature of his wicketkeeping was always the high proportion of his stumpings to his total dismissals. That year he dismissed 9 Warwickshire batsmen at Portsmouth – 4 caught and 5 stumped.

He spent most of his war service with the Army in India, and did not resume county cricket until 1920. The following year his record was superior to that of any other wicketkeeper – he made 48 catches and 34 stumpings, a grand total of 82 victims. His career prospered as he played for the Players v. the Gentlemen at Lord's and Scarborough in 1922, before being selected to tour South Africa that winter with MCC, under the captaincy of F.T. Mann. Yet, when the prospects of him succeeding Strudwick as the England wicketkeeper were at their brightest, very early in the tour he had a finger fractured while batting, and returning home missed all the tests.

In 1927, Livsey played twice for 'England' v. the Rest in the Test trial matches, but he still had not achieved international selection by the time his career ended prematurely after the 1929 season. Altogether, his victims numbered 629 over 11 full seasons, 375 of them caught and as many as 254 stumped. Was it Livsey's batting which held him back from Test selection? True, he began his career at number 11 in the order, but the first indication he gave of batting skill came in 1921, when he helped Alec Bowell in what remains a County record, 192 for the last wicket v. Worcestershire at Bournemouth. The following year he hit his first hundred in the famous match v. Warwickshire at Edgbaston when, in the follow-on after Hampshire's dismissal for 15, he and George Brown compiled 177 for the ninth wicket and Livsey scored 110 not out. He hit up 69 batting at number 10, when Phil Mead hit the highest score of his career v. Nottinghamshire in 1921. In 1928, his aggregate in County championship matches was 827 runs at an average of 22.97, including a second century of 109 not out v. Kent at Dover. That year he achieved 11 totals of over 25, including 2 fifties, his position in the batting order ranging between nine and two. However, in 1929, England's men behind the stumps were Ames or Duckworth. That June, Livsey took his benefit. Alas, it was reduced to two days by the collapse of the Surrey batting.

Livsey had become Lionel Tennyson's valet on his return from India. The arrangement does not seem to have worked to Livsey's advantage, as Tennyson's rackety, not to say dissipated, lifestyle imposed considerable strain on his physical and mental resources. As to the high quality of his performance behind the stumps however, there was never any doubt.

# Charles Bennett Llewellyn
RHB, SLA, 1899-1910

**Born:** 26 September 1876, Pietermaritzburg, South Africa

**Died:** 7 June 1964, Chertsey, Surrey

### Batting

| M | I | NO | Runs | Av |
|---|---|---|---|---|
| 196 | 341 | 23 | 8772 | 27.58 |
| 50 | 100 | ct/st | | |
| 37 | 15 | 135 | | |

### Bowling

| O | M | Runs | Wkts | Av |
|---|---|---|---|---|
| 5567.5 | 1125 | 17538 | 711 | 24.66 |
| 5wI | 10wM | | | |
| 55 | 11 | | | |

### Best Performances
216 v. South Africa, Southampton, 1901
8/72 v. Leicestershire, Leicester, 1901

Hampshire's first approach to a super-star, Llewellyn was born in Pietermaritzburg on 26 September 1876 of a father from Pembroke, Wales, and a mother born in St Helena. He excelled as an all-rounder for Natal from 1894/95 to 1897/98 before, on the recommendation of Major Poore, he emigrated to Hampshire. During the two-year qualifying period, he raised great hopes when permitted to play against the touring teams of 1899 (the Australians against whom he scored 72 and 21 and captured 8 wickets for 132 in the first innings) and 1900 (the West Indians – 93 and 6 and 13 wickets for 187) and he more than fulfilled these hopes in his first match in 1902. The opposition were his brother colonials, the South Africans, against whom he hit 216 in three hours with the aid of 30 fours and captured 4 wickets for 6 runs as the visitors suffered defeat by an innings!

That season he achieved the double – 1,025 runs and 134 wickets, but he far surpassed this bowling performance in the following year when his victims numbered 170, average 18.61; 115 of these were taken for Hampshire, whose fortunes soared, for that year at least, the whole team drawing inspiration from his performance as they rose from the foot of the championship table in 1901 to equal seventh.

His performances led in 1902 to his inclusion among the fourteen players selected for England for the First Test v. Australia at Edgbaston, although he was not included in the final eleven.

His achievements in subsequent years fluctuated, but he achieved the double feat again in 1908 and 1910. In that year, he formed a match-winning combination with the greatly improved Jack Newman, Llewellyn taking 133 wickets, average 20.45, to his partner's 156 at 18.45. They made a fine contrast, the stockily-built Llewellyn bowling left-arm slow-medium, while the wiry Newman varied fast-medium pace out-swingers with off-breaks. Twice that summer Llewellyn took 7 wickets in an innings (he achieved the feat 10 times for Hampshire) but it was the ensemble which counted most – at one period, the two men showed such deadly form that in the course of nine consecutive innings, they took all but one of their opponents' wickets, and in three successive matches they received no assistance from other bowlers.

Hampshire rose to the hitherto unscaled height of sixth in the championship, but the partnership with Jack Newman was already at an end. Llewellyn, with a growing family to support, needed greater financial stability

Charles 'Buck' Llewellyn, successful in international, county and
League cricket.

than Hampshire could afford. He left the
County and, after touring Australia in 1910/11
with the South Africans, joined Accrington in
the Lancashire League; he went on to prosper
in northern cricket for another twenty-five
years. Starting in 1895/96, Llewellyn appeared
in 15 Tests for South Africa, faring best in
1902/03, with 25 wickets, average 17.92
against Australia, and finishing rather moderately in the Triangular Tournament in 1912.

# William Geoffrey Lowndes Frith Lowndes
RHB, RM, 1924-1935

**Born:** 24 January 1898, Wandsworth
**Died:** 23 May 1982, Newbury, Berks

## Batting

| M | I | NO | Runs | Av |
|---|---|----|------|-----|
| 41 | 72 | I | 1558 | 21.94 |
| 50 | 100 | ct/st | | |
| 6 | 4 | 15 | | |

## Bowling

| O | M | Runs | Wkts | Av |
|---|---|------|------|-----|
| 528.4 | 74 | 1503 | 40 | 37.57 |
| 5wI | 10wM | | | |
| - | - | | | |

## Best Performances
143 *v.* Surrey, The Oval, 1934
3/22 *v.* Worcestershire, Worcester, 1934

Geoffrey Lowndes captained the County in 1934 and 1935, when his predecessor, Lord Tennyson, began to fade from the scene. The committee looked for an impressive personality and good cricketer who could hold his own on both counts with the likes of Alec Kennedy and Phil Mead and the rather zany collection of younger professionals who made up the team; someone who might perhaps attract some young amateurs of promise, as the appointment of a new and well-connected skipper was sometimes thought to do.

Surprising as it may seem, they found such a prodigy in Geoffrey Lowndes. He had not played much county cricket – a few games in 1924 and 1930 – but he had a cricketing lineage, in that his father, W.F.L.F. Lowndes, who had added Lowndes to his original surname of Frith, had captained Buckinghamshire from 1906 to 1912. Geoffrey himself had been two years in the Eton eleven (1915 and 1916) and after war service with the 21st Lancers in Afghanistan had been, unexpectedly, awarded his blue for the strong Oxford batting side of 1921 – he was a late choice, obtaining a trial after he showed good form against the Army scoring 88 and following this with an innings of 52 *v.* Sussex at Hove. He confirmed his right to a place in the team to play Cambridge by his performance against H.D.G. Leveson-Gower's XI at Eastbourne, where he hit up 216 and with H.P. Ward put on 218 in just over 90 minutes.

He played a good deal of good-class club cricket while farming in north Hampshire, and in 1934 did as much as could possibly have been expected of him. He hit 2 centuries in championship matches and a third and famous one *v.* the Australians at Southampton. He reached his hundred in 75 minutes and added 247 in under three hours for the fourth wicket with Phil Mead, going on to score 140 before a record crowd at Northlands Road. His figures for the 1934 season were 984 runs, average 33.93, and 32 wickets, which cost 30.09 each. No new captain could have been expected to achieve more, but there were warning signs, in that he missed half of the County's 28 championship matches. He began 1935 by hitting 118 before lunch in two hours against Kent, but made very few runs after that – the team, beset by injuries to several leading players, became easy meat for their opponents, and Lowndes retired at the end of the season.

He had perhaps been a little too old for undertaking a full season's county cricket at the age of thirty-six; John Arlott suggested that he preferred fishing! However, as his performances in 1934 showed, he was an attacking batsman and a particularly fine driver, at his best on hard, fast wickets, as well as possessing ability with fast medium away swingers and fielding ably at mid-off. Most importantly, he filled the gap caused by the inability of Tennyson to play regularly, and his two years as captain allowed time for the maturing of his successors, Dick Moore and Cecil Paris.

# Malcolm Marshall

RF, RHB, 1979-1993

**Born:** 18 April 1958, Pine, Bridgetown, Barbados

**Died:** 4 November 1999, Barbados

### Batting

| M | I | NO | Runs | Av |
|---|---|----|------|-----|
| 210 | 269 | 37 | 5847 | 25.20 |
| **50** | **100** | **ct/st** | | |
| 26 | 5 | 76 | | |

### Bowling

| O | M | Runs | Wkts | Av |
|---|---|------|------|-----|
| 6268 | 1733 | 15401 | 826 | 18.64 |
| **5wI** | **10wM** | | | |
| 45 | 7 | | | |

### Best Performances

117 v. Yorkshire, Leeds, 1990

8/71 v. Worcestershire, Southampton, 1982

The wave of grief and shock that swept the cricket world in the wake of the news of Malcolm Marshall's death in November 1999, at the tragically early age of forty-one, was felt nowhere more deeply (apart from his native Barbados) than in Hampshire. This is where he had played and coached for the best part of twenty years since arriving as a more or less raw youngster in 1979. In the course of his time with the County he had become widely acknowledged as the best – the most complete and thoughtful fast-bowler of his time, and one of the greatest of any era.

Hampshire were not a strong side when Marshall first joined them and he took a while to make an impact on the field, although he finished top of the County's averages that year – as he did in every year he played between then and 1990 except 1987. His attitude impressed from the start. But, in 1982, by which time he had established himself in the West Indies side, he had a sensational year for the County, taking 134 wickets at 15.73, including five or more in an innings on twelve occasions. Nobody had taken so many wickets in a county season since 1967, when there were far more games, and nobody has approached it since. Moreover, and this was a telling indication of Marshall's approach, nobody in the country bowled more overs; Hampshire came third in the Championship. They maintained that position in 1983 when in 16 games Marshall took 80 wickets at 16.58 (with 7 for 29 including a hat-trick, v. Somerset), and scored 563 runs at 46.91.

Within a year or so he asserted his pre-eminence as a Test match fast-bowler. At 5ft 11in he was almost dwarfed by his comrades-in-arms, Garner and Croft and, later, Ambrose and Walsh, but for five years or so from 1984 he was unquestionably the dominant figure in a formidable battery. In two series in England, in 1984 and 1988, he took 24 wickets at 18.20 and 35 wickets at 12.65.

In the 1984 series, at Headingley, he broke his left thumb batting. When the ninth West Indian wicket fell with Larry Gomes in the nineties, Marshall returned and batted one-handed to ensure that Gomes got his hundred. Incredibly, he then came out and bowled West Indies to victory, taking 7 for 53. This said all one needed to know about Marshall's approach to cricket, to his team, and to his team-mates.

There was much more to Marshall than sheer pace, though that, generated by a sprint of a run-up and a whippy arm action, was electrifying. His armoury was complete: the

Malcolm Marshall was king of fast bowlers.

outswinger, the inswinger, the leg-cutter, a lethal bouncer: he even used his relative lack of height to his advantage and was 'skiddy' in the manner of Ray Lindwall.

During the years of his prime, Marshall was unstoppable in county cricket. Mark Nicholas knew that, if a breakthrough was required, Marshall could almost always be guaranteed to deliver. This meant that from 1985 to 1990 Hampshire were usually in the running for honours. More tellingly perhaps is that when he was away in 1984 and 1988 they came fifteenth in the Championship. In 1985, when Hampshire came second in the Championship, he took 95 wickets at 17.68, and, for good measure scored 768 runs at 24.77. The following year he took 100 wickets at 15.08. In 1990 he was second in the national averages with 72 wickets at 19.18: in that year of gargantuan run-scoring, forty-five batsmen averaged over 50.

Ironically, though, in 1988 and 1991, when Marshall was again away, Hampshire not only reached Lord's for their first two one-day finals, but won the games. This was made all the more piquant by the fact that Marshall had been involved in two desperately close losing 60-over semi-finals in 1989 and 1990. Indeed, he was Man of the Match in the game v. Northamptonshire in 1990, when he scored 77 batting at number 5 and put on 141 with David Gower – Hampshire lost by one run.

His joy was palpable when Hampshire beat Kent in the 1992 Benson & Hedges final. Marshall played no small part in the victory, scoring 24 off 22 balls at the end of the Hampshire innings and taking 3 for 33.

Marshall took his batting very seriously and scored five hundreds for Hampshire, two of them coming in successive games in 1990, including his highest score of 117 v. Yorkshire, again batting at number 5 as he did for much of that year, finishing with 962 runs at 45.80.

After retiring from county cricket in 1993 he played and coached in Natal, being a mentor to such players as Shaun Pollock and Lance Klusener, and putting his vast cricketing knowledge and intuitive gift for passing on skills to effective use. Then he came back to coach at Hampshire (and for the West Indies) where a new generation of players was being given the opportunity to learn from and appreciate his exceptional talent and rare good nature.

# Roy Marshall
RHB, OB, 1953-1972

**Born:** 25 April 1930, Farmers Plantation, St Thomas, Barbados
**Died:** 27 October 1992, Taunton

**Batting**

| M | I | NO | Runs | Av |
|---|---|---|---|---|
| 504 | 890 | 49 | 30303 | 36.03 |
| **50** | **100** | **ct/st** | | |
| 161 | 60 | 232 | | |

**Bowling**

| O | M | Runs | Wkts | Av |
|---|---|---|---|---|
| 1042.2 | 363 | 2403 | 99 | 24.27 |
| **5wI** | **10wM** | | | |
| 5 | - | | | |

**Best Performances**
228* v. Pakistanis, Bournemouth, 1962
6/36 v. Surrey, Portsmouth, 1956

Of Hampshire's five outstanding post-war batsmen – Roy Marshall, Barry Richards, Gordon Greenidge, Chris and Robin Smith – Marshall had the least exposure and success at international level, and the lowest career average, well below the benchmark figure of 40.

Yet it would be a brave judge who when asked to nominate Hampshire's greatest batsman, declined to place Marshall at or adjacent to the peak. He is second only to Philip Mead in terms of runs scored and centuries made for the County and is 30th in the all-time run-making list. But it is an issue which goes beyond figures.

It is easy to forget what an impact Marshall made on county cricket from the moment of his arrival as a regular player in 1955. From the late 1960s spectators at county matches could watch strokemakers like Rohan Kanhai and Zaheer Abbas on a daily basis; they also had one-day cricket to savour. But it was not always like that. Although it was immensely popular in the years following the Second World War, and in spite, or perhaps because of the technical proficiency of its practitioners, county cricket in the 1950s and 1960s was meandering down a cul-de-sac of boredom and pointlessness as far as the outside world was concerned.

Marshall was not a part of that process. Of his contemporaries, perhaps only Dickie Dodds, David Green, Colin Milburn and Bob Barber shared Marshall's conviction that the role of the opener was to attack. Although his technique was soundly based, his method was spectacularly unorthodox. It is impossible to exaggerate either the feeling of anticipation that filled a ground when Marshall came out to bat – even Richards and Greenidge did not generate quite the same frisson – or the sense of anti-climax if he failed.

He had all the shots. Tall, bespectacled and invariably bare-headed, he was a powerful driver on both sides of the wicket and a vigorous puller. He also pioneered a stroke which is not unheard of today but which was unique in his day, the cut for six over third man.

Whatever county cricket's deficiencies at the time, it did not lack accomplished opening bowlers: Trueman, Tyson, Loader, Statham and Higgs, Jackson and Rhodes, Flavell and Coldwell – 'Marsh' took them all on. As Christopher Martin Jenkins has observed, against anyone of less than the highest class, he could be an absolute destroyer.

In his first full season with the County he made over 2,000 first-class runs and he also took 26 wickets at 11.23 with his off-breaks.

Roy Marshall – most spectacular of opening batsman.

Every year from 1958 to 1962, he scored 2,000 runs in first-class cricket and in 1959 he had a sequence of 7 successive scores of over 50. His best season was 1961, when he scored 2,607 runs at 43.45. His ability to make big scores quickly was a key factor in Hampshire winning the Championship. He made his highest Championship score, 212, in the second innings of a victory over Somerset in which Hampshire conceded a first innings lead of over a hundred. Marshall's innings contained 7 sixes and 25 fours. He and Jimmy Gray put on 155 for the first wicket – Gray's share was 38. Against Glamorgan in 1964, he scored a century before lunch on the first day's play and on three other occasions he scored a hundred or more runs in the first session of a day's play.

It was Marshall's decision as captain in 1968, to drop himself down the order and promote Richards to open. The decision was triumphantly vindicated. Richards was revealed as a world-class opener, while Marshall contributed memorable displays from the middle order. This continued after he handed over the captaincy, without noticeable enthusiasm, to Richard Gilliat in 1971. In his last season, 1972, he still averaged 41:56 and made two centuries, including a rampant 203 *v*. Derbyshire.

Marshall was Barbadian – he made his first-class debut for the island at the age of fifteen – and first came to Hampshire's notice when he made a marvellous 135 against them for the West Indians at the County Ground in 1950. There was no place for the twenty-year-old Marshall in that immensely strong batting line-up, but he played two Tests each against Australia and New Zealand in 1951/52. Then, after playing league cricket, he threw in his lot with Hampshire, despite having to spend two years qualifying and effectively ruling himself out of Test cricket. While qualifying he had an outstanding game against the 1953 Australians, taking 4 for 69 and making 71 (out of 148) on a very difficult wicket.

There must have been times when Marshall wondered whether he had made the right decision. That is suggested by the title of his autobiography, *Test Outcast*. Be that as it may, Michael Manley in his *History of West Indies Cricket* mentioned the view that Marshall and Gordon Greenidge were the two most accomplished openers produced by the West Indies. Marshall took immense pride in playing for his adopted county. It is good that the newly-named 'Marshall Drive' was named to commemorate two great Hampshire Barbadians.

# Rajesh Maru

RHB, SLA, 1984-1998

**Born:** 28 October 1962, Nairobi, Kenya

**Batting**

| M | I | NO | Runs | Av |
|---|---|---|---|---|
| 213 | 216 | 55 | 2818 | 17.50 |
| **50** | **100** | **ct/st** | | |
| 7 | - | 240 | | |

**Bowling**

| O | M | Runs | Wkts | Av |
|---|---|---|---|---|
| 6394 | 1807 | 16948 | 504 | 33.62 |
| **5wI** | **10wM** | | | |
| 15 | 1 | | | |

**Best Performances**

74 v. Gloucestershire, Gloucester, 1988
8/41 v. Kent, Southampton, 1989

Raj Maru, who hailed from Nairobi by way of Brent, was a canny and intelligent cricketer who bowled slow left-arm, batted stubbornly and was a quite brilliant close fielder. He was seldom short of a word of advice for friend or foe – initially under the helmet but subsequently at slip where in both Championship and limited-overs cricket he held some superb catches. He took seven in a match v. Northamptonshire in 1988, equalling the county record. Had he been guaranteed a regular place in the side, Maru would have been a plausible candidate to succeed Mark Nicholas as captain.

By then, he was only making periodic appearances in the Championship in what were increasingly trying times for county spinners but he did enjoy one memorable game v. Warwickshire in 1996 when Hampshire outplayed the reigning champions. Acting captain Robin Smith was injured in Hampshire's first innings and Maru led the team in the field, his captaincy being praised in the *Wisden* match report. The game was also memorable for a passage of play when Maru bowled over the wicket and outside leg stump (a young Ashley Giles was playing for Warwickshire) to Dermot Reeve, the Warwickshire captain, who responded by throwing his bat away to avoid being caught off lifting deliveries.

Maru came to Hampshire down a well-trodden path from Middlesex and at once lent a new dimension to the county's attack. His heyday was in the mid-1980s and the early 1990s and he was the leading spinner in the Championship side from 1985 to 1991. He started modestly in 1984 when Hampshire, shorn of their West Indian stars, were relatively weak, but like many of the County's spinners he prospered at Bournemouth, taking 2 for 24 and 4 for 23 in a win over Sussex and 7 for 79 against Middlesex. In 1985, when Hampshire came second in the Championship he took 73 wickets at 26.34; v. Gloucestershire, again at Bournemouth, he took 5 for 16 in 12 overs in a low-scoring win. In 1987, he took 66 Championship wickets at 29.34 and he was a solid contributor for the next couple of years. In 1989, he had the best bowling performance of the season, and his career, 8 for 41 (12 for 105 in the match) v. Kent.

Nigel Cowley had tended to be preferred in the one-day side initially: thus Maru did not feature at all in the Sunday League title-winning side in 1986. Oddly he played in only one of Hampshire's three one-day finals, v. Surrey in the NatWest in 1991. His contribution may not look significant in the scorebook – six overs for 23 runs, a catch and 1 not out – but his coolness under pressure as a late-order batsman as the run-chase reached its climax was beyond statistical measurement.

Raj Maru is now a member of the County's coaching staff.

# Dimitri Mascarenhas

RFM, RHB, 1996 to date

**Born:** 30 October 1977, Chiswick

### Batting

| M | I | NO | Runs | Av |
|---|---|-----|------|------|
| 86 | 128 | 13 | 2678 | 23.28 |
| 50 | 100 | ct/st | | |
| 13 | 2 | 34 | | |

### Bowling

| O | M | Runs | Wkts | Av |
|---|---|------|------|------|
| 1941.4 | 543 | 5534 | 176 | 31.44 |
| 5wI | 10wM | | | |
| 5 | - | | | |

### Best Performances

104 v. Worcestershire, The Rose Bowl, 2001
6/26 v. Middlesex, The Rose Bowl, 2001

'Dimi' was born in London, raised in Australia and came to Hampshire in 1996 on the recommendation of Paul Terry. He began inauspiciously with a 'duck' and match figures of 0-77 for the Second XI but performed steadily through the season and on 3 September he made his first-class debut in sensational style at Northlands Road. After the Glamorgan openers had scored 177 for the first wicket against Renshaw, Thursfield, Maru and Botham, Mascarenhas dismissed them both and although the Welsh side made 401 he had figures of 32-8-88-6, the best debut bowling figures for the County in the twentieth century. He took 3-62 in the second innings and 7-147 in the next match at Canterbury and looked to have the brightest future.

This was emphasised when he took five wickets in his first bowl of the following season at Oxford, but he made little progress in 1997. In 1998 he established himself as an all-rounder in all competitions and was awarded his county cap. His value in limited-overs cricket was emphasised in an excellent performance in the NatWest semi-final v. Lancashire at Southampton. He took 3-28 in Lancashire's 60 overs total of 252 and with Hampshire's reply in ruins at 28-5 he top-scored with 73 in a valiant but vain effort to reverse their fortunes. He made less progress in a full season in 1999, but in 2000 at Derby he shared a sixth-wicket partnership of 187 with Kenway and recorded his maiden first-class century. Sadly Hampshire had their first experience of relegation that year, but 'Dimi' enjoyed 4-25 in a NatWest quarter-final success at Lord's and continued to perform well in the new 45-over National League.

In 2001, he marched to the wicket with Hampshire 79-6, in the inaugural first-class match at the Rose Bowl and he became its first centurion. He also took Hampshire's first wicket on the ground and with 6-60 v. Derbyshire and 6-26 in the successful promotion 'decider' v. Middlesex, he appeared to like his new home. He was used with varied success as a pinch-hitter in some league games but became a very frugal opening bowler in the competition.

'Dimi' offers an exotic dimension and a sparkling smile to Hampshire's cricket but he is also a thoroughly professional cricketer with the determination of an Australian upbringing and a temperament for the big occasion. At the time of writing (2003), he is a key member of the Hampshire side and still under twenty-five, so there is no reason why he should not take his career a stage further – at least in limited-overs cricket.

# Neil McCorkell ————————————————————————

RHB, WKT, 1932-1951

**Born:** 23 March 1912, Portsmouth

**Batting**

| M | I | NO | Runs | Av |
|---|---|---|---|---|
| 383 | 675 | 63 | 15833 | 25.87 |
| **50** | **100** | ct/st | | |
| 76 | 17 | 514/176 | | |

**Bowling**

| O | M | Runs | Wkts | Av |
|---|---|---|---|---|
| 29.3 | 6 | 117 | 1 | 117.00 |
| **5wI** | **10wM** | | | |
| - | - | | | |

**Best Performances**

203 v. Gloucestershire, Gloucester, 1951
1/73 v. Cambridge University, Cambridge, 1950

Neil McCorkell was born in Old Portsmouth in 1912 and learned his cricket at Portsmouth Town School and for the Portsmouth Brotherhood. Hampshire needed a new wicket-keeper to replace George Brown and McCorkell made his debut in the second game of 1932 at Taunton. In the following match, v. Nottinghamshire at Southampton, he conceded no byes and made his first dismissals including four stumpings off the bowling of spinners Jim Bailey and Stuart Boyes. Bailey took 7-7 in the second innings but Hampshire were dismissed for 57 and 30 and lost heavily.

The percentage of dismissals by stumping has declined dramatically in the past fifty years. This is not simply a reflection of ability but a measure of major changes in the way first-class cricket is played. Neil McCorkell is second to Bobby Parks in the County's dismissals list with 688 but he stumped over one hundred more batsmen than Parks – principally from the slow bowling.

McCorkell's 68 dismissals in 1932 were enough to earn him a county cap. It is a salutary thought that no Portsmouth-born, state-educated cricketer has achieved that feat in the subsequent seventy years. At the end of the season, the *Hampshire Guide* observed that 'he has the right temperament for county cricket, and he has a bright future.'

The prediction was apposite. He made his first half-century v. Yorkshire in July 1933 and in 1935 Hampshire promoted him to open the batting. He was not an immediate success, but towards the end of July he top-scored in both innings v. Lancashire at Southampton including

his first century. He repeated the feat in the next match at Liverpool and after two half-centuries scored a third hundred at Bournemouth in August. From then on, he was that most useful team-member, a batting wicketkeeper and over the next ten seasons he scored 14 more hundreds and a career total of 15,833 runs. He reached 1,000 runs in a season 9 times.

McCorkell appeared for the Players at Lord's in 1936 and at the end of the following season toured India in a team captained by Lord Tennyson. He was just twenty-seven when the war arrived and he was on a permanent night-shift building the Spitfires which helped to bring the peace. He gave little thought to cricket and struggled for runs when play resumed in 1946. After the war he was one of five players to share a joint benefit between 1948 and 1950 – the individual figure of £1,470 being a club record for the time.

He said that, 'wicketkeeping was my prime work', although, during his final seasons he was sometimes replaced in that role by Harrison, Prouton or the amateurs, D.E. Blake or C.J. Andrews. Nonetheless, he continued to open the batting with Neville Rogers and in June 1951 made his highest score, 203 at Gloucester. At the end of that season, he moved to South Africa as a coach, where he still lives. In 1952, *The Hampshire Handbook* paid tribute to 'his efficiency, his modesty [and] his lack of fuss', adding that 'Hampshire cricket is much the poorer for his going.'

# H.C. McDonnell
RHB, RLB, 1908-1921

**Born:** 19 September 1882, Wimbledon, Surrey
**Died:** 23 July 1965, Onich, Fort William,
Inverness

**Batting**

| M | I | NO | Runs | Av |
|---|---|----|------|-----|
| 78 | 120 | 12 | 1747 | 16.17 |
| 50 | 100 | ct/st | | |
| 6 | - | 69 | | |

**Bowling**

| O | M | Runs | Wkts | Av |
|---|---|------|------|-----|
| 1609.4 | 194 | 5901 | 263 | 22.43 |
| 5wI | 10wM | | | |
| 11 | 1 | | | |

**Best Performances**
76 v. Somerset, Taunton, 1913
7/47 v. Somerset, Southampton, 1914

Harold Clark McDonnell was a juvenile prodigy, successful both at Winchester and Cambridge as a leg-break bowler and was also a useful bat. He won light blues in 1903, and the two following seasons. In 1904, his successful bowling v. Surrey (15 wickets for 138) led to his selection for that County. With another brilliant schoolboy, the eighteen-year-old J.N. Crawford, he bowled unchanged v. Gloucestershire at Cheltenham, McDonnell's share being 10 wickets for 89. No wonder that Hampshire were glad to make room for him in 1908 in the holidays, when he was a master at Twyford School. He proved particularly effective in 1909, when his wickets, in little more than a month's cricket, numbered 48, at an average of 21.39. With six wickets for 22 in the match, he played a large role in the dismissal of Warwickshire for 48 and a 7-wicket win for Hampshire in 1912. His best analysis for the County was 7 for 47 v. Somerset at Southampton in 1914, when he headed the bowling averages with 35 wickets, at an average of 17.40. He continued this good form in August 1919 when first-class bowlers were in

short supply, securing 9 wickets for 143 in the match with Gloucestershire at Bristol, and a week or so later, 8 wickets for 103 v. Somerset at Bournemouth, providing substantial relief for Alec Kennedy, who that season bowled three times as many overs as anyone else in the side. McDonnell was a very good man to come in in the second half of the batting order: he could produce a dour defence or hit hard as the state of the game demanded. When he made his highest score for Hampshire, 76 against Somerset at Taunton in 1913, he and Jack Newman added 134 in an hour and a half, and as late as 1919, he hit up 64 out of 104, in partnership with A.J.L. Hill against Middlesex. He dropped out of the team after the 1921 season. McDonnell became headmaster of Twyford School. A bachelor, he was a shy and withdrawn man, looked after by his sister; on his retirement, he married and went to live in the north of Scotland. It had been said of him that he only really unwound when excelling at all forms of sport – and snowballing, which may account for his high reputation as a fielder, especially to his own bowling, allegedly once bringing off a caught and bowled dismissal at short leg!

# C.P. Mead
LHB, SLA, 1905-1936

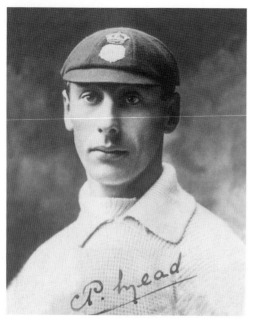

**Born:** 9 March 1887, Battersea, London
**Died:** 26 March 1958, Boscombe, Bournemouth

**Batting**

| M | I | NO | Runs | Av |
|---|---|----|------|-----|
| 700 | 1171 | 170 | 48892 | 48.84 |
| 50 | 100 | ct/st | | |
| 231 | 138 | 629 | | |

**Bowling**

| O | M | Runs | Wkts | Av |
|---|---|------|------|-----|
| 2983.4 | 626 | 9252 | 266 | 34.78 |
| 5wI | 10wM | | | |
| 5 | - | | | |

**Best Performances**
280* v. Nottinghamshire, Southampton, 1921
7/18 v. Northamptonshire, Southampton, 1908

Somebody once suggested to John Arlott that Phil Mead's interest in cricket was limited to batting. 'No, not even batting', came the reply, 'only scoring runs.' Runs in profusion accrued to Mead between 1905 and 1936. Only Jack Hobbs, Frank Woolley and Patsy Hendren have exceeded his career total of 55,061 runs and only Hobbs, Hendren and Wally Hammond have bettered his 153 centuries. Among Hampshire players he stands alone and he always will now that the counties' programmes have been so greatly reduced. In terms of runs per innings, Barry Richards and C.B. Fry both exceeded his career average for Hampshire (47), but Richards played only ten full seasons for Hampshire compared with Mead's 27, while Fry's cricket for the County was limited to 44 matches over seven summers astride the First World War.

Yet the limitation implied by John Arlott's comments stands up to examination: Mead's skills as a left-arm bowler began to be apparent during his first engagement with Surrey as a fifteen year old in 1902. He was a fairly regular member of the Hampshire attack until his batting reached full maturity in 1911 (in 1908 he recorded figures of 7 for 18 which led to an astonishing victory over Northants), but then he stopped taking it seriously – he was a fast

outfield with a low whippy return, but after 1919 reserved his running for movement between the wickets. He was a very reliable slip fielder until his later years, taking 629 catches for Hampshire, but he was not as nimble as the more dashing Frank Woolley. Mead played 17 Test matches for England; Woolley's Tests numbered 64 including 52 consecutive appearances between 1909 and 1926, but he retained his skills as a slow left-armer until the mid-1920s. In 1911, Mead and Woolley were rivals for a place in the England eleven, but following the MCC tour to Australia in the following winter, it was Woolley who gained the favour of the selectors. Although Mead had many swiftly hit innings to his name, Woolley became world famous from 1911 onwards for the splendour of his stroke play which could change the course of a match in the passing of half-an-hour, an important consideration when Test matches in England were limited to three days.

For Hampshire, Mead's high scoring seemed as extraordinary at the time as it still does now. On eleven occasions between 1911 and 1934, he exceeded 2,000 runs in a season, twice going on to overtop the 3,000. Three times, in 1921, 1926 and 1933, he hit 10 hundreds in a season and in a fourth summer,

1928, they actually totalled 13. Annual harvests of other seasons included 9 centuries in a season, twice, 8 twice and 7 three times. On 11 occasions, he scored over 200 in an innings, the highest being 280 not out *v.* Nottinghamshire at Southampton in 1921 when, in the words of a veteran spectator, he stonewalled all day! In fact, that innings included 1 six and 32 fours. It remains the third highest individual innings ever recorded for Hampshire. Three times he hit a hundred in each innings of a match, and he scored three hundreds in consecutive innings; on the first occasion, in 1921, his scores were the 280 not out *v.* Notts, and 113 and 224 *v.* Sussex at Southampton. The last instance came in 1933 when he was in his forty-seventh year. In 1935, when he was for the first time for many years, pressed into service to open the batting *v.* Notts at Trent Bridge when the County were three men short because of illness or injury, he carried his bat through the foreshortened innings for 117 not out. In 1911, he achieved a purple patch, hitting a hundred runs before lunch on the third day *v.* Warwickshire at Southampton and speeding to 207 not out in the course of only three hours' faultless batting, with the aid of 32 fours. The next day he hit another hundred before lunch and advanced his total to 194, made out of 292, and again hitting 32 fours, 401 runs for once out, in two consecutive days! Fourteen years later, he added a hundred to his total before lunch on the third day *v.* Worcestershire.

The number of high partnerships which he shares with colleagues was legendary, ranging from two of 193 for the first wicket in 1910, both with Jimmy Stone, the wicketkeeper, through 250 for the second with A.C. Johnston *v.* Warwickshire at Coventry in 1912, 344 with George Brown *v.* Yorkshire at Portsmouth in 1927 for the third wicket, and another seven stands over 180. Further large stands for each wicket include for the seventh, 270 with J.P. Parker *v.* Kent at Canterbury in 1926, 178 for the eighth with C.O. Brutton in 1925, 197 for the ninth, his partner W.R. de la C. Shirley in 1923, and 122 with Stuart Boyes for the last wicket in 1922. Nearly all of these resulted from determined back-to-the-wall

Concentration displayed in every line. Phil Mead around 1925.

batting which often saved the side after early failures.

Many of his runs came from firm strokes on the leg side or 'pushing' through the covers, which found the gaps and reached the boundary. He counselled against hitting the ball too hard, or in the air, although he was not beyond doing so if the field was placed too close. Yet it is true that spectators watching his progress with half an eye would be surprised as he reached each milestone – 50, 100, 150 in such a short space of time – without any apparent effort. What spectators did remember was his practice before receiving the ball: facing square leg, he would touch the peak of his cap three times, turn and take three little steps to the crease, and tap his bat three times in the block hole. He would hold up any bowler who tried to interrupt the process and go through the whole ritual again before facing the next delivery. He was retired from the County side early in 1937 but enjoyed two highly successful seasons for Suffolk in 1938 and 1939. However, during the Second World War his sight deteriorated and for the last dozen years of his life he was virtually blind, a disability which he met with stoicism.

**Born:** 1 February 1964, Winchester

**Batting**

| M | I | NO | Runs | Av |
|---|---|---|---|---|
| 105 | 179 | 16 | 5665 | 34.75 |
| 50 | 100 | ct/st | | |
| 24 | 13 | 78 | | |

**Bowling**

| O | M | Runs | Wkts | Av |
|---|---|---|---|---|
| 39.2 | 3 | 241 | 5 | 48.20 |
| 5wI | 10wM | | | |
| - | - | | | |

**Best Performances**
221 v. Surrey, Southampton, 1992
2/41 v. Kent, Canterbury, 1991

A technically proficient opening batsman who seemed ideally suited to four-day cricket, Tony Middleton's finest hour came in a limited-overs match, the NatWest trophy final against Surrey in 1991. Hampshire had only recently learned that Chris Smith, whose record in the competition was second to none, would not be playing. The Winchester-born Middleton had not featured in the earlier rounds, although he had done well in the Benson & Hedges Cup earlier that year. He seized his chance and stood firm against the onslaught of Waqar Younis at the beginning of Hampshire's pursuit of a target of 241, putting on 90 with Paul Terry and 70 with Robin Smith. Middleton's 78 played a crucial part in Hampshire's victory.

He had made his debut in 1984, but competition was intense in the early days to break into Hampshire's strong batting line-up. In 1990 he was given an opportunity by an injury to Kevan James and made the most of it, scoring 1,238 runs at 47.61 in what was admittedly a batsman's summer. Against Northamptonshire at Bournemouth he put on 292 for the first wicket with Terry.

The NatWest performance not surprisingly seemed to give him a boost and in 1992 he was easily Hampshire's leading run-scorer with 1,780 runs at 49.44 with 6 centuries, and 7 other scores of over fifty. With Chris Smith gone, he was the regular opener and he and Terry put on 246 for the first wicket v. Sussex in the opening game of the season. Within a month he made his highest score, 221 v. Surrey putting on 267 with Terry. In the next game, v. Lancashire, he made 73 (putting on 164 for the first wicket with Kevan James) and 138 not out. Hampshire won all three games. He also headed Hampshire's Sunday League averages with 592 runs at 59.20 and shared another solid opening partnership with Terry in the Benson & Hedges Cup final win over Kent.

In some ways, Middleton's outstanding season in 1992 was the worst thing that could have happened. It resulted in his selection for the England 'A' tour of Australia, where he had a disastrous time. That was bad enough but it seemed to affect his confidence on coming back to county cricket in 1993, when his returns were extremely modest.

In 1995, Tony Middleton was appointed Hampshire's cricket development officer and he went on to do invaluable work as the County's Second XI coach, guiding them to the Championship title in 2001. As a member of the club's cricket committee, he remains a key figure in Hampshire's future.

# Richard Henry Moore

RHB, RM, 1931-1939

**Born:** 14 November 1913, Bournemouth
**Died:** 1 March 2002, Llanrhos, North Wales

**Batting**

| M | I | NO | Runs | Av |
|---|---|----|------|-----|
| 129 | 225 | 7 | 5885 | 26.99 |

| 50 | 100 | ct/st | | |
|----|-----|-------|---|---|
| 19 | 10 | 114 | | |

**Bowling**

| O | M | Runs | Wkts | Av |
|---|---|------|------|-----|
| 285.1 | 42 | 978 | 25 | 39.12 |

| 5wI | 10wM | | | |
|-----|------|---|---|---|
| - | - | | | |

**Best Performances**
316 v. Warwickshire, Bournemouth, 1934
3/46 v. Sussex, Worthing, 1937

Dick Moore was a combative sportsman and a forceful personality, who achieved cricketing fame as a very young man. He learned his cricket at Bournemouth School and did so well in local club cricket that he received his initial trials for Hampshire in 1931, when he was only seventeen years old. A determined performance against the bowling of Larwood and Voce, bowlers for Nottinghamshire and England, ensured further opportunities in the next two seasons. Dick Moore achieved little and probably thought that Hampshire had seen the last of him for the season in the middle of 1933; it was only because Phil Mead's varicose veins caused him to withdraw from the side to play Essex at Bournemouth that Moore regained his place. He made the most of his opportunity, hitting a bold innings of 159 against an attack including Morris Nichols, Ken Farnes and Peter Smith (all present or future England bowlers), during almost four hours of bold aggression, which included 20 fours.

In 1934, still only twenty years old, he became a regular member of the Hampshire team, and he soon rose to the position of opener with John Arnold. Against Sussex, when he was second out, he had amassed 137 out of Hampshire's 249 and v. Somerset he equalled that total of 159. By the end of 1934 his total of runs was 1,569, with an average of over 30. Then ill luck intervened: in May 1935, he was stricken by scarlet fever and

missed the whole of the remainder of the season. The following winter he was appointed captain of Hampshire. His strong and aggressive personality proved highly popular with his side of mostly young players. They rose to the occasion with such success that at the beginning of August they found themselves third in the championship table. Then poor results in August resulted in them finding themselves tenth at the end of the season. Moore's aim at a definite result might have been successful in 1937 but for a succession of injuries, in particular to the left-arm bowlers, Boyes and Creese. Only in the Bournemouth week in July were the County at full strength, and they won both games. In the first, v. Warwickshire, Moore achieved immortality. First, he hit a hundred before lunch, achieving the feat with a six off the last ball of the morning and after a quiet start on the resumption, he launched into a dazzling array of drives, hits to leg and delicate late cuts. In 6 hours and 20 minutes he scored 316, which overtook Robert Poore's 304 v. Somerset in 1899. In Hampshire's next match, v. Surrey, he scored another century, and by the end of the season his total number of runs was 1,553 although following this successful season, he was called to the family business and resigned the captaincy.

Playing as often as he could in 1938, he hit three centuries to finish at the head of the County's averages with 770 runs in 17 innings at an average of 45.29. This swansong (for he played only three games in 1939) only accentuated the sense of loss among the County's supporters. Never a man to look back, he became a leading figure organising cricket festivals at Colwyn Bay, chairing the club, and acting as groundsman when the need arose.

# Alan Mullally
LHB, LFM, 1988-2002

**Born:** 12 July 1969, Southend-on-Sea, Essex

**Batting**

| M | I | NO | Runs | Av |
|----|----|------|------|------|
| 35 | 40 | 12 | 196 | 7.00 |
| 50 | 100 | ct/st | | |
| - | - | 6 | | |

**Bowling**

| O | M | Runs | Wkts | Av |
|--------|-----|------|------|-------|
| 1274.2 | 396 | 3125 | 157 | 19.90 |
| 5wI | 10wM | | | |
| 12 | 1 | | | |

**Best Performances**
36 *v.* Derbyshire, Derby, 2001
9/93 *v.* Derbyshire, Derby, 2000

England's best left-arm pace bowler since John Lever, Alan Mullally has added much needed variety to Hampshire's attack over the last few years. By the time he joined Hampshire, he was a master of the art of swinging the ball into the right-hander, without which the left-arm pace bowler is unlikely to trouble the best batsmen. He played a valuable role in seeing the County to promotion to the first division of the County Championship for 2002.

Mullally was the less expensive part of the injection of talent that was intended to revolutionise Hampshire in the 2000 season. But, like Shane Warne, Mullally could hardly be blamed for the calamity that ensued. On the contrary, they both did all that could have been asked of them: between them they did much to ensure that Hampshire obtained maximum bowling bonus points. Mullally, signed from Leicestershire (he had played one game for Hampshire in 1988) took 49 Championship wickets at 16.97 in only eight matches. He only played in three home Championship games, taking 3 for 38 and 2 for 12 as Durham were beaten at Basingstoke, 6 for 75 *v.* Surrey and 5 for 84 and 4 for 59 *v.* Leicestershire; Hampshire still lost both the latter games. At Derby he took a career best 9 for 93 – 14 for 188 in the match.

2001 was a happier season all round and again

Mullally performed admirably, taking 52 first-class wickets at 17.50 including 5 or more wickets in an innings six times. He was at his most incisive in late July and early August. In the historic win over the Australians he took 5 for 18 before lunch on the first day when the visitors were bowled out for 97 and he followed this up with 8 for 90 *v.* Warwickshire. This earned him a recall to the England side for the Fourth Test at Headingley. Unfortunately, he appeared less than fully fit and, not for the first time at the highest level, put in a strangely diffident and tentative performance. Even so, he was able to claim the unique distinction of having been in two teams that beat the 2001 Australians.

More surprising than Mullally's omission from the Test side was his exclusion from England's one-day international squad given that, at the end of the 2001 English season, he was ranked as the fourth best one-day international bowler in the world. It may be that perceived shortcomings in the field and with the bat have had something to do with this. Still, not everyone has to watch their cricket through Fletcher-tinted spectacles – and nobody who watches Mullally bat and field would trot out the tedious mantra that there are no characters left in cricket.

If Mullally's international career is indeed over, he looks an even better signing for Hampshire now than he did in 2000, assuming the County can retain his signature and his commitment.

# John Alfred Newman
RHB, RFM/OB, 1906-1930

**Born:** 12 November 1884, Southsea, Hants
**Died:** 21 December 1973, Cape Town,
South Africa

**Batting**

| M | I | NO | Runs | Av |
|---|---|----|------|-----|
| 506 | 786 | 121 | 13904 | 20.90 |
| **50** | **100** | **ct/st** | | |
| 62 | 9 | 295 | | |

**Bowling**

| O | M | Runs | Wkts | Av |
|---|---|------|------|-----|
| 16046.2 | 3227 | 48305 | 1946 | 24.82 |
| **5wI** | **10wM** | | | |
| 128 | 34 | | | |

**Best Performances**
166* v. Glamorgan, Southampton, 1921
9/131 v. Essex, Bournemouth, 1921

Jack Newman was the only one of the big four – Mead, Brown, Newman and Kennedy – to have been born in Hampshire. He was also the only one to conceal his real date of birth during his playing career (he knocked four years off when he joined the County). He enjoyed major triumphs from almost his earliest days, taking 8 for 54 and 5 for 66 for Hambledon v. an England team on Broadhalfpenny Down in 1908, which raised his season's total to 93 wickets. He improved on this analysis the next season when he actually dismissed 8 of M.A. Noble's Australians for 43, including one hat-trick, the other two batsmen being run out. That year Newman's victims numbered 89, which paled into insignificance in comparison with his performances in 1910, when he and Charles Llewellyn carried all before them, capturing 289 wickets between them, Newman's share being 156. He took seven wickets in an innings four times that year, the opposition including Yorkshire and Warwickshire, both strong batting sides. By 1912, he and Alec Kennedy were established in a bowling partnership which lasted for 18 years, and reached its climax in the years 1921 to 1923 – Jack

Newman contributed 177 victims in 1921, 122 in the following year, and 148 in 1923. Taking wickets became harder work as the 1920s wore on, but Jack Newman achieved the double of 1,000 runs and 100 wickets in 1926 and the two following years; three fine seasons. He took 145 wickets in 1926, when his all-round performance v. Gloucestershire almost defied belief – scores of 66 and 42 not out, and with the ball, 8 wickets for 61 and 6 for 87; v. Northants he had match figures of 3 for 1 and 8 for 30 – 11 wickets for 31. The following year, he hit a century in each innings v. Surrey at the Oval, and took eight wickets in both Somerset innings at Weston-super-Mare. He and Alec Kennedy twice bowled unchanged in each innings of a match v. Sussex in 1921, and Somerset two years later, both performances at Portsmouth. He took 100 wickets in a season on eight occasions, and performed the double of 1,000 runs and 100 wickets five times.

Jack Newman was lean, taut, a man of moods. By the 1920s with so much depending on him and Kennedy, he was opening the bowling with sharp swingers, when the shine had gone off the ball he turned to off-spin,

A cartoon of John Newman.

varied by a vicious one which went with his arm, sometimes defeating wicketkeeper and slips as well as bat. A few seasons were mostly frustrating for him, but he was still an integral member of the side, with 638 runs and 81 wickets in 1930. Then, heeding medical advice, he retired and became a first-class umpire. He then coached in South Africa where he died at the (real) age of eighty-nine.

Two thousand wickets, but John Newman never played for England.

**Born:** 29 September 1957, London

### Batting

| M | I | NO | Runs | Av |
|---|---|----|------|-----|
| 361 | 597 | 85 | 17401 | 33.98 |
| **50** | **100** | **ct/st** | | |
| 77 | 34 | 207 | | |

### Bowling

| O | M | Runs | Wkts | Av |
|---|---|------|------|-----|
| 948.5 | 169 | 3163 | 69 | 45.84 |
| **5wI** | **10wM** | | | |
| 2 | - | | | |

### Best Performances
206* v. Oxford University, Oxford, 1982
6/37 v. Somerset, Southampton, 1989

When Mark Nicholas handed over the reins to John Stephenson towards the end of the 1995 season, he was in his eleventh year as captain of Hampshire. That makes him third on the list in terms of longevity after Lionel Tennyson and Desmond Eagar and compared with the brief tenures currently in vogue for county captains it seems a vast length of time.

Nicholas did indeed seem to be something of a throwback to a bygone era. Although modern and professional in everything he did, there was something of the air of the old-fashioned amateur about him. There was a hint of this in the circumstances of his appointment as captain. Nicholas, of Bradfield, was chosen to succeed Pocock, of Shrewsbury, ahead of Jesty, of Privet Secondary Modern. His manner, his easy charm, his communication skills, even his hair, seemed to set him apart. The hauteur with which he saw to the reversal of an umpiring decision that had gone against him, in a game against the 1992 Pakistan tourists, had to be seen to be believed.

The 'love him or hate him' reaction of the viewing public to Nicholas as, in all fairness, a polished, knowledgeable and enthusiastic presenter of cricket on Channel 4, is doubtless a reflection of his standing in the closeted and inward-looking world of first-class cricket. But the length of his tenure at Northlands Road, and the success Hampshire enjoyed under him are a measure of the regard in which he was held in the County. He may have had an affable manner but Nicholas could read the riot act when necessary and he was a shrewd and positive leader.

In those eleven years, Hampshire won four one-day titles, the Sunday League in 1986 and three finals – he was personally mortified to miss the 1991 NatWest final through injury. Hampshire's non-appearance in a Lord's final had become something of a burden – there were NatWest semi-final losses in 1988, 1989 and 1990, the last two agonisingly close. Nicholas seemed to have thrown off that hoodoo, although there was another near miss in the Benson & Hedges Cup in 1994.

In the Championship, Hampshire came second in 1985, third in 1990 and were out of the top six only once in the years between. For seven of his eleven years in charge (from 1985 to 1993, except for 1988 and 1991) Nicholas, as he would be the first to acknowledge, could call upon the services of the world's greatest bowler. But even Nicholas could not arrange for Malcolm Marshall to bowl from both ends. In 1985, when Hampshire came second, Maru and Tremlett both took more than 70 first-class wickets to

go with Marshall's 95 but in the following year, when Marshall took 100 wickets, nobody else took 50. They often seemed a bowler short of Championship material.

The splendid side of the late 1980s and early 1990s gradually disintegrated with the departure, for various reasons, of Tremlett, Chris Smith, Ayling, Gower and Marshall. Nicholas never lost his keenness, or his conviction that the next bright young prospect would make the difference. If the side he handed over to John Stephenson was not as good as the one he had inherited, it was not for lack of enthusiastic leadership.

Nicholas was a very good County batsman, better than his figures suggest, and he scored 34 hundreds in his eighteen years with the county. In the mid-1980s he was frequently spoken of as an England candidate, but he lacked the consistency to break through into the Test side. He had a thin time of it between 1990 and 1993 when he was suffering the effects of a bout of malaria contracted while leading England 'A' in Zimbabwe. At his best, he was a good-looking batsman with a wide range of strokes. In 1994 he finished top of Hampshire's batting averages and in his final year, 1995, he was the only batsman to score 1,000 Championship runs for the County.

Nicholas now has as high a public profile as any former Hampshire player has ever had. Apart from his television jobs, he is one of the most literate former cricketers in the press box. As a member of the MCC committee and a key figure in the restructured Hampshire set-up, Mark Nicholas' influence on the English game may still be in its infancy.

# David O'Sullivan

LHB, SLA, 1971-1973

**Born:** 16 November 1944, Palmerston North, New Zealand

### Batting

| M | I | NO | Runs | Av |
|---|---|----|------|-----|
| 26 | 31 | 9 | 347 | 15.77 |
| **50** | **100** | **ct/st** | | |
| - | - | 14 | | |

### Bowling

| O | M | Runs | Wkts | Av |
|---|---|------|------|-----|
| 982.4 | 396 | 2001 | 84 | 23.82 |
| **5wI** | **10wM** | | | |
| 5 | 1 | | | |

David O'Sullivan is the bowler in this photograph.

### Best Performances

45 *v.* Somerset, Taunton, 1973

6/26 *v.* Nottinghamshire, Bournemouth, 1973

David O'Sullivan, a slow left-arm bowler from Palmerston North in New Zealand, took fewer than a hundred wickets for Hampshire over the three seasons in which he played for the County. Yet to exclude him from a book of this sort would be churlish and even bizarre, for it is likely that without O'Sullivan, Hampshire would not have won the Championship for the second time in 1973.

He had taken 29 wickets in eleven Championship matches in 1972 and he started the 1973 season in the side but lost his place to an extra batsman, either Richard Lewis or Andy Murtagh (Hampshire used only thirteen players in the campaign). When Hampshire beat Lancashire at Southport on 27 July, they returned to the top of the table where they remained for the rest of the summer. By a quirk of the fixture list, their remaining six games were all at home and as the pitches got dryer through August, O'Sullivan became indispensable. He finished with 47 Championship wickets at 20.59. In the last six games alone he took 33 wickets at 13.75.

As in 1961, Hampshire won the Championship using two left-arm spinners. Peter Sainsbury and O'Sullivan complemented each other perfectly, the New Zealander being a much bigger spinner of the ball and having a beautiful 'loop'.

Against Essex at Portsmouth, normally a seamers' paradise, he took 6 for 35 in the second innings as the visitors narrowly averted an innings defeat. In the second game of the Portsmouth Week he took 4 for 60 in 38 overs in the first innings against Derbyshire and Sainsbury was the destroyer in the second. In the crucial game *v.* Northamptonshire at the County Ground, O'Sullivan took 4-50 in the second innings – Sainsbury did not bowl a ball in the match – and then Nottinghamshire were routed as O'Sullivan claimed 6 for 26 and 3 for 8 at Bournemouth. In the second innings of the final game of the season *v.* Kent at Southampton, he took 5 for 93. He also contributed useful runs from number 9 in some of these matches.

That Kent game was O'Sullivan's last for Hampshire. Forced by the hardly ungenerous rules on the signing of overseas players to choose between O'Sullivan and West Indies fast-bowler Andy Roberts, the County opted for Roberts.

O'Sullivan remained a prolific wicket-taker in New Zealand and played in four Tests for his native country.

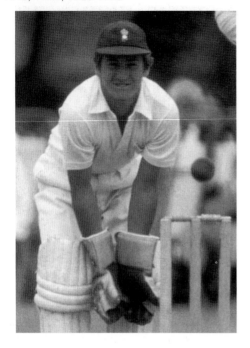

**Born:** 15 June 1959, Cuckfield, Sussex

Batting

| M | I | NO | Runs | Av |
|---|---|----|------|-----|
| 253 | 282 | 82 | 3936 | 19.68 |
| 50 | 100 | ct/st | | |
| 14 | - | 630/70 | | |

Bowling

| O | M | Runs | Wkts | Av |
|---|---|------|------|-----|
| 31.3 | 1 | 166 | 0 | - |
| 5wI | 10wM | | | |
| - | - | | | |

**Best Performances**
89 v. Cambridge University, Cambridge, 1984

Cricketing pedigree does not get much better than that of Bobby Parks, Hampshire's boyish-looking wicketkeeper throughout the 1980s. His father, J.M. Parks, was a distinguished Test player, his grandfather, J.H. Parks, played Test cricket and is the only man to have made 3,000 runs and taken 100 wickets in a season, while great-uncle H.W. Parks was a good enough player to have scored over 20,000 runs for Sussex.

Bobby Parks came as close to playing for England as it is possible to do without actually being selected. On a bizarre day at Lord's in 1986, in the First Test against New Zealand, when Bruce French was injured, Parks was the officially endorsed 'substitute'. He would never have let England down. He was a 'natural' wicketkeeper, neat and agile if undemonstrative, and capable of marvellous glovework – his stumping of Curtly Ambrose in the 1990 NatWest semi-final lives in the memory.

Parks came into the side in 1980, and remained Hampshire's first-choice wicketkeeper until the closing weeks of the 1990 season. In 1986, he had 81 dismissals, putting him second on Hampshire's all-time list.

Parks was consistently near the top of the national list for dismissals throughout the 1980s, finishing second in 1982 and 1989. In 1982, Malcolm Marshall took 134 wickets as Hampshire came second in the Championship. Parks took 25 catches off Marshall's bowling.

In 1981, his first full season, he overtook Walter Livsey's record, set in 1914 by taking 10 catches in a match v. Derbyshire – it remains Hampshire's record in the Championship. His 6 catches in the first innings also equalled the Hampshire record and he twice equalled it himself later.

Parks was a handy batsman at number 8 or 9. Of his many useful partnerships, arguably none was more crucial than that with Kevan James v. Surrey in the 1986 Sunday League, which enabled Hampshire to set a defendable target and win the title. Against Nottinghamshire in the Championship the following year, he and James put on 152 for the eighth wicket, Parks scoring 62 not out. Batting must, however, have been a factor when he lost his place to Adi Aymes towards the end of the 1990 season. It must have been a blow to Parks, who was still only thirty-one. He had one last hurrah, appearing in the Benson & Hedges final against Kent in 1992. He remains Hampshire's leading wicketkeeper with the statistically satisfying record of 700 dismissals, including 70 stumpings.

# Nick Pocock
RHB, 1976-1984

**Born:** 15 December 1951, Mara Caibo, Venezuela

**Batting**

| M | I | NO | Runs | Av |
|---|---|---|---|---|
| 127 | 186 | 22 | 3790 | 23.10 |
| 50 | 100 | ct/st | | |
| 18 | 2 | 124 | | |

**Bowling**

| O | M | Runs | Wkts | Av |
|---|---|---|---|---|
| 92.2 | 18 | 396 | 4 | 99.00 |
| 5wl | 10wM | | | |
| - | - | | | |

**Best Performances**
164 v. Lancashire, Southampton, 1982
1/4 v. Sussex, Portsmouth, 1979

Had he played only one game for the County, Nick Pocock might still have merited a footnote in its history as the only Hampshire player to have been born in Venezuela. Had he captained the county for only one season – his first as captain was 1980 – he would have been granted a longer, if less cheerful, mention as the only Hampshire captain since 1905 to have led his side to the wooden spoon in the Championship. But Pocock led Hampshire for five years and, in two of them, 1982 and 1983, they came third in the Championship. Thus he has to be placed in the top half a dozen Hampshire captains both in terms of longevity and success.

Pocock epitomised the amateur spirit more than any of Hampshire's other post-war captains including the two amateurs, Desmond Eagar and Colin Ingleby-Mackenzie. He made his debut aged twenty-four, in 1976 – scoring 68 v. Leicestershire at Bournemouth. He played only a handful of games in that and the next few seasons, on leave not from the Army or the Church, or school-mastering, as he might have been in pre-war times, but from Ingleby-Mackenzie's insurance business.

In 1979, under Bob Stephenson's captaincy, he scored 393 runs at 19.65, which did not suggest that the now twenty-seven-year-old Pocock would have a glittering cricket career ahead of him. However, he did play one splendid innings

of 143 not out v. Middlesex at Portsmouth. Gordon Greenidge made 145, Pocock came in at 152 for 4 added 74 for the fourth wicket with Greenidge – no other Hampshire batsman made more than 18.

Even so, outsiders must have been surprised when Pocock was appointed to replace Stephenson as captain in 1980. Without the West Indian contingent for almost the whole season, the County slipped to bottom place. Pocock played in every game and scored 874 runs at 23.62.

Things could only get better. The County came a thoroughly respectable seventh in 1981 with Greenidge and Marshall back in harness. In 1982 they came third and Pocock made his highest score of 164 v. Lancashire at Southampton. They maintained that position in 1983 – Pocock again played in all the games and scored 755 runs at 27.96. He had a good team and in Malcolm Marshall an exceptional bowler, but Pocock was an enterprising leader and he played his part in Hampshire's success – the team also put in solid performances in the Sunday League in those years.

In 1984, with Greenidge and Marshall away again Hampshire slumped to fifteenth in the Championship and by mid-season Pocock had effectively retired.

# Major R.M. Poore
RHB, Lobs, 1898-1906

**Born:** 20 March 1866, Carysfort, Dublin
**Died:** 14 July 1938, Bournemouth

## Batting

| M | I | NO | Runs | Av |
|---|---|----|------|-----|
| 36 | 66 | 7 | 2819 | 47.77 |
| 50 | 100 | ct/st | | |
| 9 | 10 | 23 | | |

## Bowling

| O | M | Runs | Wkts | Av |
|---|---|------|------|-----|
| 26.2 | 2 | 100 | 3 | 33.33 |
| 5wI | 10wM | | | |
| - | - | | | |

## Best Performances
304 v. Somerset, Taunton, 1899
1/9 v. Sussex, Southampton, 1902

In 1899, Robert Montague Poore stunned the cricket world with a succession of long scores. Between 12 June and 12 August in 21 innings, he cut and drove 1,551 runs at an average of 91.23, his 21 innings realising 7 centuries and three other scores over fifty. He began with two hundreds in the match v. Somerset at Portsmouth, followed with a third from the Lancashire attack at Southampton, and a fortnight later took a 'well nigh perfect' 175 from the Surrey bowlers at Portsmouth. By this time, his performances had attracted nationwide attention but small scores for the Gentlemen v. the Players, 1 and 24 at the Oval and 27 in the big match at Lord's, brought a diminution in his quickly-made reputation. But this did not last long. On 20 July at Taunton, when Hampshire replied to Somerset's score of 315, Poore went in to bat at 5.45 p.m. and by the close of play, he had contributed 24 not out The next day, Poore reached his century in one hour and 55 minutes. When his partner, Tom Soar, was caught for a career best of 95, they had put on 196 in 115 minutes. This was only the prelude to a marvellous feast of hitting as Poore, joined by Captain E.G. Wynyard, passed his 150 and proceeded to treat all the bowling alike. By tea, the Hampshire total was 261 for 5, Poore 216 and Wynyard 106. The 600 arrived after 405 minutes batting. At 298, Poore was badly missed, but he had reached 304 when he was at last stumped. In the meantime, he had lost Wynyard for 225 after four hours and twenty minutes' batting in which the pair had added 411, the highest partnership for any wicket, except the first in first-class cricket. His

innings comprised 2 fives, 45 fours, 6 threes and 7 twos. Last out, Poore batted six hours and fifty minutes. In the fortnight or so of cricket which remained to him, Poore made 29 and 71 v. the Australians and finished his season with 157 and 32 at Leicester. Soon he was engulfed in the South African war, and only when it ended in May 1902 was he able to return to first-class cricket.

He did not renew his form of 1899 and when he returned, aged forty, in 1906, he injured his leg, and the century which he scored in spite of his handicap turned out to be his last innings for the county.

Poore's great performances of 1899 did not come out of a clear blue sky – he scored well for Bombay Presidency in the early 1890s, and his play for South Africa against a touring English side in 1895/96 gained him a good trial in 1898 with MCC and Hampshire, when he hit 2 centuries and scored 735 runs at an average of 28.

Robert Poore excelled in all the sports which the Army had to offer: fencing, polo, tent pegging, racquets, and even lemon cutting. In that summer of 1899, he was named the Best Man at Arms at the Military Tournament. He is still remembered for his spring cricket coaching classes, and his continuing skill with the bat, which in club cricket lasted well into his sixties.

# A.E. 'Sam' Pothecary

LHB, SLA, 1927-1946

**Born:** 1 March 1906, Southampton
**Died:** 21 May 1991, Uxbridge, Middlesex

## Batting

| M | I | NO | Runs | Av |
|---|---|----|------|-----|
| 271 | 445 | 39 | 9477 | 23.34 |

| 50 | 100 | ct/st | | |
|----|-----|-------|---|---|
| 47 | 9 | 146 | | |

## Bowling

| O | M | Runs | Wkts | Av |
|---|---|------|------|-----|
| 517.5 | 64 | 2140 | 52 | 41.15 |

| 5wI | 10wM | | | |
|-----|------|---|---|---|
| - | - | | | |

### Best Performances
130 v. New Zealanders, Bournemouth, 1937
4/47 v. Surrey, The Oval, 1927

They called him Sam after his uncle, who played a little for Hampshire either side of the First World War. A long-term supporter of Hampshire said, 'they really played him for his fielding, you know – he and Johnnie Arnold were brilliant on the off-side', but this does less than justice to Sam's batting. In the early 1930s, opposition bowlers were confronted by a cluster of highly idiosyncratic left-handed batsmen for Hampshire – George Brown, Phil Mead, Jim Bailey, Len Creese and Sam Pothecary junior. Sam, a member of the nursery established in the mid-1920s, first played for Hampshire in 1927 v. Surrey at the Oval. He captured four wickets in Surrey's second innings, including both openers, Jack Hobbs and Andrew Sandham. He never fulfilled his early promise as a slow left-arm bowler, but by 1932 he had established himself in the Hampshire team. In 1933, he reached 1,000 runs for the first time, 1,216 runs at an average of 27.

His best seasons were 1936, 1937 and 1938. In 1936, he hit 100 v. Northamptonshire at Portsmouth – batting at the lowly position of number 9. His highest score came the following year – 130 v. the New Zealand tourists at Bournemouth, and that same season he hit up 118 in 90 minutes v. Gloucestershire at Portsmouth, adding 160 with Johnnie Arnold. His total that season, 1,309 runs, he exceeded

in 1938 when his performances earned him 1,357 runs in a summer when only he and Neil McCorkell really performed consistently with the bat.

Like so many cricketers who could see storm clouds ahead, he was below par in 1939. Although appointed senior professional for 1946, he appeared in only three matches before retiring. From 1949 to 1958, he was a first-class umpire, before becoming groundsman at the Royal Air Force ground at Vine Lane, Uxbridge. On his retirement in 1975, he was presented with a substantial cheque, an inscribed silver salver, a Hampshire CCC Coalport 1973 Championship plate, and an illuminated address showing the names of the contributors.

By 1975, he had had forty-eight years' involvement in cricket as player, umpire, and groundsman, with only ten of them spent as a full-time member of the Hampshire eleven. Watching him compile a fifty or a hundred in the latter role, you might think him a world beater as he played a succession of sparkling shots on the offside, but he was vulnerable to the short ball on the offside or the off-ball swinging in, so his final figures were no more than 9,477 runs, at an average of 23.34. As a fielder at cover point, in particular, or anywhere on the off-side, he was world-class, but he was certainly not played just for his fielding.

# John Rice

RFM, RHB, 1971-1982

**Born:** 23 October 1949, Chandlers Ford, Hants

### Batting

| M | I | NO | Runs | Av |
|---|---|---|---|---|
| 168 | 271 | 22 | 5091 | 20.44 |
| **50** | **100** | **ct/st** | | |
| 22 | 2 | 153 | | |

### Bowling

| O | M | Runs | Wkts | Av |
|---|---|---|---|---|
| 2822.4 | 718 | 7707 | 230 | 33.50 |
| **5wI** | **10wM** | | | |
| 3 | - | | | |

### Best Performances

161* v. Warwickshire, Birmingham, 1981
7/48 v. Worcestershire, Worcester, 1977

John Rice was a tall (6ft 3in), rather gangling right-handed all-rounder whose mop of fair hair and loping gait made him a distinctive figure in the Hampshire ranks between 1971 and 1982. He was happy to bat up or down the order as the needs of the team dictated and would nag away with his steady right-arm medium-pace, occasionally opening the bowling, but usually first or second change.

Rice established himself in 1975. He had a useful year in the first-class game, scoring over 600 runs and taking 49 wickets. It was in the one-day game though, that he really made an impact. Hampshire won the Sunday League, their first one-day title, and Rice bowled most overs and took most wickets (27) at the lowest average (11), taking 5 for 14 (including a hat-trick) in a 10-over thrash v. Northamptonshire. He turned in another solid performance in 1978 when the County won the title for a second time, holding 16 catches in the season – a record in the competition and five in the match v. Warwickshire.

In 1977 he took 44 first-class wickets, including a career-best 7 for 48 v. Worcestershire in a game Hampshire won by 6 wickets. In the previous game he had taken 5 for 31 as Hampshire beat Essex by an innings. In 1979 he took 5 for 17 v. Warwickshire; Hampshire won by 290 runs – Rice had helped Gordon Greenidge put on 97 for the first wicket in Hampshire's first innings.

By this time, Rice was becoming more useful as a batsman than a bowler. In that year he finished with 927 runs, many of them scored as an opener, and although he had a poor 1980, marred by fitness problems, he came back strongly as a batsman in 1981, making 639 runs at 39.93 in eleven games. In September, he made his highest score, 161 not out v. Warwickshire. In the previous game, v. Sussex, he went in after Tim Tramlett had fallen to the first ball of the match and 'carried his bat' for 101 out of 241.

Rice scored almost 800 runs as an opener, and held 26 catches, mostly at slip, in 1982 but he was not re-engaged at the end of the season. Rice signalled his view of the news by depositing his bat in a waste-paper bin on his way back to the dressing room.

John Rice has spent many years in charge of cricket at Eton College.

# Barry Richards
RHB, OB, 1968-1978

**Born:** 21 July 1945, Durban, South Africa

**Batting**

| M | I | NO | Runs | Av |
|---|---|----|------|-----|
| 204 | 342 | 33 | 15607 | 50.50 |
| 50 | 100 | ct/st | | |
| 91 | 38 | 264 | | |

**Bowling**

| O | M | Runs | Wkts | Av |
|---|---|------|------|-----|
| 618 | 194 | 1675 | 46 | 36.71 |
| 5wI | 10wM | | | |
| 1 | - | | | |

**Best Performances**
240 v. Warwickshire, Coventry, 1973
7/63 v. Rest of the World, Bournemouth, 1968

You do not have to have been a Hampshire supporter of the 1960s and 1970s to believe that Barry Richards was one of the outstanding batsmen of the twentieth century – Sir Donald Bradman, no less, put him in his all-time world eleven. But Hampshire, for whom he scored almost half his 28,358 first-class runs (average 54.74) and 34 of his 80 centuries, could claim to have seen the better part of him.

Whether Richards shared that view at the time is debatable. For many people, a shadow was cast over his career by the sense of disillusionment, described in his autobiography, that characterised the final phase of his time with the County and led to his departure in the middle of the 1978 season.

Such disenchantment was understandable. More than any other truly great player, Richards was a victim of time and circumstance. The ban on sporting contacts with South Africa limited his Test career to four games against Australia in 1969/1970 – a series that South Africa won 4-0. Richards's scores were 29 and 37, 140, 65 and 35, and 81 and 126. Apart from the games between the Rest of the World and England in 1970 and World Series Cricket, that was the limit of his exposure at international level. So, this sublimely-talented player had to parade his gifts on the more modest stage of County (and provincial and State) cricket. 'It's too easy',

Neville Cardus quotes Walter Hammond as saying, after gorging himself on County attacks. There must have been times when Richards felt something similar.

He joined Hampshire in 1968 when the restrictions on the registration of overseas players were relaxed. Richards had spent a summer playing for Gloucestershire Second XI with his friend Mike Procter, and had earlier toured England with a South African schools team, so he was not a totally unknown quantity. Even so, few could have anticipated what a sensational signing he would be – except Richards himself. He said he would score 2,000 runs in the season, and he was as good as his word. In only his second match, against the champions, Yorkshire, at Harrogate, on a cold day and in difficult conditions, he made 70 out of 122 batting at number 4 and playing, according to his own assessment twenty years later, as well as he ever did throughout his career.

Richards did not look back after that. Swapping places in the batting order with Roy Marshall, he finished the season as the country's leading run-scorer with 2,395 runs. Hampshire were fifth in the Championship,

Second only to Don Bradman.

the first time they had finished in the top nine since winning the title in 1961. Two centuries in a game v. Northamptonshire and a double century v. Nottinghamshire were among the highlights. Richards, an off-spinner described by Peter Sainsbury as the most talented slow-bowler to play for Hampshire during his time at the County, also took 7 for 63 v. a Rest of the World side at Bournemouth.

For six seasons between 1971 and 1977, Richards opened with Gordon Greenidge – together they could be a devastating pair and the weight and pace of their run-getting played an important part when Hampshire

won the Championship in 1973. There were some notable contributions from Richards, including 240 v. Warwickshire, his highest score for Hampshire (he made 356, 325 in a day, for South Australia v. Western Australia). None of the large crowd who were present on the thrilling last (second) afternoon of the game against leading challengers, Northamptonshire, will forget Richards's 37 not out – out of 90 for 3 – a masterly display according to *Wisden* – to lead Hampshire to victory when Bishan Bedi was threatening to run through the side.

In the curtain-raiser at Lord's the following season, he made 189 out of 249 for 6 against a strong MCC attack. Later that month, he made 225 not out, out of 344, v. Nottinghamshire, putting on 202 for the seventh wicket with Mike Taylor who made 68. No other Hampshire player made double figures and there were only three scores of over 20 in Nottinghamshire's two innings. On three occasions he carried his bat through a Hampshire innings, scoring 127 not out of 192 v. Northamptonshire in 1970.

One could go on. The figures are impressive, but it is almost an insult to mention them in connection with a batsman as gifted, both aesthetically and technically, as Richards. Indeed the smaller innings, the 30s and the 40s, were often as memorable as the big ones. He made it all look so simple. And then suddenly, nobody could tell how or why, he would be on his way back to the pavilion. The fact is that very few county bowlers 'got' Richards out. However mundane the cricket he played seemed to him, he adorned the county game in a way that few players have achieved in its history.

# Andy Roberts
RHB, RF, 1973-1978

**Born:** 29 January 1951, Urlings Village, Antigua

### Batting

| M | I | NO | Runs | Av |
|---|---|----|------|-----|
| 58 | 65 | 23 | 583 | 13.88 |
| 50 | 100 | ct/st | | |
| - | - | 11 | | |

### Bowling

| O | M | Runs | Wkts | Av |
|---|---|------|------|-----|
| 1784.1 | 526 | 4076 | 244 | 16.70 |
| 5wI | 10wM | | | |
| 13 | - | | | |

### Best Performances
39 v. Northamptonshire, Bournemouth, 1975
8/47 v. Glamorgan, Cardiff, 1974

Andy Roberts was the first in the line of great West Indian fast-bowlers who dominated world cricket from the mid-1970s to the early 1990s. Malcolm Marshall was the greatest fast-bowler to play for Hampshire, but in terms of sheer menace even he might have had to yield first place to Roberts. A tall and powerful man, Roberts was fearsomely quick and had a lethal bouncer. He went about his work in an unnervingly dispassionate manner, rarely smiling or snarling. Martin Crowe, the New Zealand master batsman, wrote of the challenge involved in facing Roberts, emerging 'shaking and white', albeit unbeaten, from a short-pitched barrage. He was talking about 1984, ten years after Roberts first traumatised county batsmen.

In 1973, when Hampshire won the Championship, Roberts had been confined to the Second XI; reports suggested that medical attention was regularly needed to revive the afflicted and they were only the batsmen waiting in the dressing room. In 21 games in 1974 Roberts took 119 wickets at 13.62, figures which even Marshall would have been proud of. Hampshire won 9 of their first 13 games, 4 of them by an innings, 1 by ten wickets and 1 by nine wickets. Roberts's influence in these wins cannot be exaggerated – there is no doubt that his presence at one end facilitated the capture of wickets at the other.

Against Kent at Basingstoke, he took 4 for 12 in 15 overs and 5 for 27; v. Sussex at Bournemouth 3 for 25 and 5 for 41; 3 for 54 and 6 for 27 v. Northamptonshire at Northampton – 3 for 17 and 4 for 29 against the eventual champions, Worcestershire at Portsmouth, 8 for 47 (including a spell of four wickets in five balls) v. Glamorgan, at Cardiff in a game Hampshire lost.

The following year in 13 games – he was absent on World Cup duty – he took 57 wickets at 15.80 as Hampshire 'slumped' to third. As in 1974, he was top of the national averages. A match haul of 5-33 and 4-44 v. Lancashire at Liverpool was a highlight. In 1977, troubled by an ankle injury and sometimes apparently short of motivation, he took 40 wickets at 19.

But 1974 was the year to remember. He had some notable scalps – almost literally, in those helmet-less days. At different ends of the age-scale, Colin Cowdrey was simultaneously out cold and out hit wicket at Basingstoke, while in a memorable Benson & Hedges quarter-final, Ian Botham, batting at number 9 was hit in the face, but batted on, minus several teeth, to win the game for Somerset.

Roberts was probably over-bowled by Gilliat (who could blame him?) and relations deteriorated in the course of 1978, Roberts leaving the County in the middle of the season to concentrate on World Series Cricket. He subsequently played part-time for Leicestershire.

**Born:** 20 June 1859, Twickenham, Middlesex
**Died:** 27 September 1943, Abingdon, Berks

**Batting**

| M | I | NO | Runs | Av |
|---|---|----|------|-----|
| 129 | 230 | 14 | 3299 | 15.27 |
| **50** | **100** | **ct/st** | | |
| 8 | 1 | 165/37 | | |

**Bowling**

| O | M | Runs | Wkts | Av |
|---|---|------|------|-----|
| 31 | 1 | 143 | 1 | 143.00 |
| **5wI** | **10wM** | | | |
| - | - | | | |

**Best Performances**
101 v. Warwickshire, Birmingham, 1900
1/40 v. Sussex, Hove, 1900

Robson's career figures give no idea of his value to Hampshire over their first seven or eight years in the County Championship. He kept wicket or took any position in the field and, indeed, any position in the batting order as need arose. He also stood in as captain until he was formally appointed to the post in 1900, at a time when the County's fortunes were at their lowest. He moved to Southampton in the mid-1880s, after 12 matches with Middlesex, and played for Hampshire in their earliest championship match in 1895. He was then an ever-present in the team until 1902, witnessing their varied fortunes during the early years and the dreadful decline when the military were called away for service in the Boer War – a year after he took on the burden of the captaincy. In that year, 1900, no fewer than 41 individuals turned out for Hampshire (28 of them bowled) in their 22 matches, of which 16 were lost and the remainder drawn. Under the system of points which applied then, they achieved minus 16! Robson played 37 innings, scoring 545 runs at 16.02, only four more or less regular members of the side averaged over 20.

Charles Robson had one day of glory that summer when at Edgbaston he hit his maiden century in first-class cricket in his forty-first year, and shared in a big stand with E.M. Sprot, enabling Hampshire for once that season to claim an honourable draw. He must have been a happier man in 1901, when strengthened by the presence of C.B. Llewellyn and J.G. Greig, the County rose to seventh in the championship with 7 victories compared to their 6 defeats. Robson himself hit 405 runs in championship matches at an average of 15. He sometimes opened the innings and at least once batted at number 11. That successful season made a fine climax to Robson's career; 1902 provided an anticlimax when the County slumped again to the foot of the table. E.M. Sprot was ready to take over the captaincy and Robson resigned.

A large, cheerful man, he was well-known in business circles in Southampton where his company manufactured soft drinks, and like other contemporaries who were involved with Hampshire cricket, he was also closely associated with football. He was secretary of Southampton FC when they played at the Antelope ground, and was on the board of management when the club moved to the Dell.

In club cricket, he was a prolific scorer who shared in many large stands with C.B. Fry at the training ship *Mercury*. His popularity is reflected by his selection on a tour of the USA, and for the first official MCC tour of Australia in 1903/4, under P.F. Warner, when Robson was the reserve wicketkeeper – a great compliment to a highly-tried, if ageing, player.

# Neville Rogers
RHB, 1946-1955

**Born:** 9 March 1918, Oxford

### Batting
| M | I | NO | Runs | Av |
|---|---|----|------|-----|
| 285 | 506 | 25 | 15292 | 31.79 |
| 50 | 100 | ct/st | | |
| 73 | 26 | 194 | | |

### Bowling
| O | M | Runs | Wkts | Av |
|---|---|------|------|-----|
| 4.4 | 0 | 37 | 0 | - |
| 5wl | 10wM | | | |
| - | - | | | |

### Best Performances
186 *v.* Gloucestershire, Portsmouth, 1951

Neville Rogers arrived at Southampton as a twenty-one year old at the start of the 1939 season, having followed the path from Oxford established by such impressive predecessors as Alec Bowell, George Brown, Johnny Arnold and 'Lofty' Herman. He was unable to play first-class cricket because of the stringent qualification rules then in force.

It was 1946 before the full debut came. Neville served overseas throughout the war, and can remember just one game of cricket. When the news of a contract arrived, he was equally relieved and uncertain as to his ability. Nonetheless, he joined his colleagues in repairing the County Ground before appearing at number 6 *v.* Worcestershire in the first match. Four wickets fell fairly cheaply after which Neville joined his lifelong friend Jim Bailey and they added 209 together. No player has ever made a century for Hampshire on their first-class debut – on this occasion Neville fell 10 short.

He did not sustain that form in his first season in the middle order, but the following year he was promoted to open, generally with Arnold or McCorkell. His first game at the top of the order was *v.* Sussex and having reached 99, Jack Nye had him lbw. There would be four more dismissals in the 90s before his first century *v.* Cambridge University at Portsmouth (generally a happy ground) and 2 further hundreds followed rapidly.

With the senior players like Arnold and McCorkell reaching the end of their careers, Neville quickly established himself as Hampshire's key batsman. The County was not strong, but Neville's form was such that he was selected for a Test trial and as twelfth man for England in 1951. In the following game for Hampshire he hit a century *v.* the touring South Africans, but the Test cap never came.

In 1954 he equalled the record of carrying his bat four times in one season and he also captained Hampshire for the first time. In the following season Roy Marshall and Jimmy Gray established their vital opening partnership. Neville dropped to number 5 but, at last, enjoyed playing in a successful side as Hampshire secured their highest-ever position of third. The end of the season was especially sweet for Neville as he captained the side in their last 5 Championship matches, winning 4 and drawing 1.

At the age of thirty-seven he sought the security of a three-year contract and a benefit. Hampshire offered just one year and by the time they revised their offer, Neville had obtained a post in a company with his old pal Jim Bailey. It is a measure of the man that, having given his word, he turned his back on the game he loved. It is equally typical that after retirement he gave his time to support his friend Jimmy Gray in his role as cricket chairman at Northlands Road.

# Peter Sainsbury

RHB, SLA, 1954-1976

**Born:** 13 June 1934, Chandlers Ford, Hants

## Batting

| M | I | NO | Runs | Av |
|---|---|---|---|---|
| 593 | 913 | 189 | 19576 | 27.03 |
| 50 | 100 | ct/st | | |
| 96 | 7 | 601 | | |

## Bowling

| O | M | Runs | Wkts | Av |
|---|---|---|---|---|
| 14273.3 | 5823 | 30060 | 1245 | 24.14 |
| 5wI | 10wM | | | |
| 35 | 5 | | | |

## Best Performances

163 *v.* Oxford University, Oxford, 1962
8/76 *v.* Gloucestershire, Portsmouth, 1971

Hampshire may have had more flamboyant players, but they have had few more loyal servants than Peter Sainsbury – only Philip Mead and Alec Kennedy have played more than his 593 first-class games for the county, for whom he also served as coach for several years after his retirement. He was the only man to appear in both Hampshire's Championship-winning teams and he was a key member of each.

Sainsbury took 102 wickets at 18.50 with his slow left-armers in 1955, his first full season, after playing just seven games in 1954. On his twenty-first birthday, he twice dismissed Len Hutton as Hampshire beat Yorkshire in Yorkshire for the first time since 1932 and he took 5 for 40 as they beat the champions Surrey in the penultimate game of the season.

Sainsbury's reward for his efforts in 1955 was a berth on the MCC 'A' tour to Pakistan in 1955/56. Whatever the reason, he was not quite the same bowler on his return from that tour. Sainsbury was never a great spinner of the ball and his success in 1955 was largely attributable to his use of flight. After the Pakistan tour he started to push the ball through more and became a rather negative bowler and rarely a match-winner. He regularly picked up 50, 60 or 70 wickets a season, but seldom struck terror in the hearts of opposing batsmen.

Suddenly, however, he rediscovered the secret of flight and guile. In 1971, at the age of thirty-seven, he had the best season of his life, taking 107 wickets at 17.51 and scoring 959 runs at 33.06 with 9 fifties. Once again he was winning matches for Hampshire with the ball, taking 11 wickets in the victory over Yorkshire – including 6 for 14 in the second innings. On seven occasions he took five or more wickets in an innings, including 8-76 (in a total of 192 for 9) *v.* Gloucestershire. In his last season, 1976, he took 66 wickets at 18.72.

Before 1971, Sainsbury's batting had arguably become more important to Hampshire than his bowling. He had his limitations as a batsman – in a career of over twenty years in which he scored over 20,000 runs he made only 7 centuries. Even his warmest admirers would not claim that he was an especially attractive batsman. After watching Marshall or Richards destroy an opposition attack it could almost be said that a pall was cast over proceedings as 'Sains' walked swiftly to the wicket, determined, it seemed, to put a stop to all the nonsense. His primary objective appeared to be to work every delivery, if humanly possible, through mid-wicket.

Yet the fact is that Sainsbury, despite spending a large part of his career batting at number 6 and below, did score those 20,000 runs. When the top order failed, Sainsbury

Peter Sainsbury (centre) with Mervyn Burden (left) and Mike Barnard goes out to field at Dean Park, Bournemouth.

was always there to pick up the pieces. He scored a thousand runs in each season from 1960 to 1964 and in 1967. And it would be unfair to suggest that he was a slow scorer. His superb athleticism meant that he could always keep the scoreboard moving with quick singles and there is no denying the vigour of his on-side strokeplay.

His batting and bowling did not give the full picture, however. Peter Sainsbury was one of the outstanding fielders of his generation. Only 7 post-war players have taken more than his 617 catches in first-class cricket. A high proportion of these were taken in the leg trap, but Sainsbury's expertise there was not exclusive – he was a fine outfielder too. Once his remarkable ability was recognised, he saved many runs by reputation alone. But it was his close catching that will be remembered, and he formed a lethal combination with Derek Shackleton.

Sainsbury's value can be seen in his contribution to the two Championship titles. In

1961 he scored 1,459 runs at 31, took 54 wickets at 26 and held 46 catches. In 1973 he was even more influential. By then he was vice-captain. He finished third in the batting averages scoring a century v. Somerset, his first for nine years. He topped the bowling, (coming second in the national averages) with 49 wickets at 17.73. Against Sussex at Southampton he took 6 for 29 in 29 overs in the first innings and 3 for 45 in 48 overs in the second. His slow-bowling partnership with David O' Sullivan was critical to Hampshire's success.

Peter Sainsbury never represented his country: it seems extraordinary now, with the dearth of quality slow-bowlers and all-rounders. The cupboard was far from bare in Sainsbury's time and he has had to content himself with being, perhaps with Derek Morgan of Derbyshire and Hampshire's Jack Newman, the best all-rounder never to have played for England.

**Born:** 12 August 1924, Tormorden, Yorkshire

### Batting

| M | I | NO | Runs | Av |
|---|---|---|---|---|
| 583 | 773 | 177 | 8602 | 14.43 |
| **50** | **100** | **ct/st** | | |
| 17 | - | 207 | | |

### Bowling

| O | M | Runs | Wkts | Av |
|---|---|---|---|---|
| 24466.5 | 8936 | 48674 | 2669 | 18.23 |
| **5wI** | **10wM** | | | |
| 190 | 37 | | | |

### Best Performances
87* v. Essex, Bournemouth, 1949
9/30 v. Warwickshire, Portsmouth, 1960

'Hampshire without Shackleton will be like Blackpool without its Tower.' So said *Wisden*, reporting the retirement of the phenomenal Derek Shackleton, at the end of the 1968 season. This was scarcely an exaggeration. In each year from 1949 'Shack' had taken at least 100 wickets for the county. Only Yorkshire's Wilfred Rhodes achieved that feat more often and nobody, including Rhodes, has done it – or ever will – in twenty consecutive seasons. Against Somerset at Weston in 1955 he took 8 for 4 in seven overs and followed it up with 6 for 25 in the second innings. On three occasions in England since 1935 two bowlers have bowled unchanged through both completed innings of a match and Shackleton was involved in two of them. He finished with 2,857 first-class wickets, eighth on the all-time list, one place behind Alec Kennedy – although, for Hampshire alone, Shackleton finished ahead.

All this was achieved with an apparent effortlessness that defied logic. Shackleton would walk out to take the new ball at 11.30 in the morning, immaculately groomed and turned out, and walk off again at 6.30 p.m. – if the opposition lasted that long – as though he had strolled round the corner to post a letter rather than bowled 38 overs and taken 5

for 80. In his twenty-one-year career with Hampshire, Shackleton yielded slightly over two runs an over.

A number of ingredients made up this remarkable package. His unrivalled longevity and consistency as an opening bowler could partly be put down to exceptional fitness – he rarely missed a game through injury and apart from being grey-haired he looked much the same in his last season as he had in his first. If anything he improved as he got older – after 1960 his average for a Championship season never reached as high as twenty. He had a wonderfully economical action – a smooth, light twelve-yard run-up and a classically high arm. Never more than medium-fast even once he had settled down to his new role as a seamer (he came to Hampshire as a leg-spinning all-rounder and became a pace bowler almost by accident), his strengths were relentless accuracy and immense subtlety of variation in terms of swing, seam and cut. It was his wrist action that gave his bowling deceptive pace off the pitch. Then there was his temperament, being the most unflappable and patient of opening bowlers.

His accuracy, in terms of both length and line, was a by-word. If 'Shack' bowled a half volley or a long hop, it used to be said, the county committee went into emergency conclave. This almost metronomic quality could very occasionally make him susceptible to

'Shack', a useful all-rounder, steers one past the slips.

spontaneous outbursts of unorthodox hitting. In the first game of the 1958 season *v*. Yorkshire, Colin Ingleby-Mackenzie opted to bat first and declared in an attempt to get first-innings points in a game ruined by rain. In these unusual, not to say bizarre circumstances, Yorkshire reached 106 for 3 in thirteen overs. Fred Trueman scoring 68 not out: Shack took 0-64 in seven overs.

Occasionally it was said – most publicly by Denis Compton in a *Wisden* article – that Shackleton was a negative bowler. This was unfair. His principal method of keeping runs down was to take wickets. He also happened to be extremely difficult to score off. The fact is that Shack was a match-winner in county cricket and one of the most feared bowlers in the country, as *Wisden* said in its report on the 1961 season, when Shackleton bowled in excess of 1,500 overs and took 158 first-class wickets at 19.09. Twelve times in that year he took five or more wickets in an innings, none more important than his spell in Derbyshire's second innings in the penultimate Championship game. Ingleby-Mackenzie has said that Shack was the crucial factor in winning the Championship.

He was born in Todmorden and served in the Pioneer Corps during the war – a more combative role was ruled out by poor eyesight. Indeed one of the most extraordinary things, and best-kept secrets, about Shackleton was that he was effectively blind in one eye.

He played just seven Tests between 1950 and 1963, presumably because there were doubts about how effective he would be on Test pitches against Test batsmen. At least he had the consolation of playing in one of the greatest of all, against West Indies' at Lord's in 1963. He finished off the West Indies first innings by taking three wickets in four balls and featured as a batsman (he was a useful all-rounder in his younger days, failing by only 86 runs to do the double in 1949 and scoring 42 not out in his first Test) in the thrilling finale. He lost a dramatic if slow-motion sprint to the non-striker's end to fellow veteran Frank Worrell.

Blackpool without its Tower? Shack came back for one Championship match in 1969 *v*. Sussex at Portsmouth. Opening the bowling in the week before his forty-fifth birthday, he sent down 47.5 overs and took 2 for 37 and 5 for 58.

# Chris Smith
RHB, OB, 1980-1991

**Born:** 15 October 1958, Durban, South Africa

### Batting

| M | I | NO | Runs | Av |
|---|---|---|---|---|
| 222 | 383 | 48 | 15287 | 45.63 |
| **50** | **100** | **ct/st** | | |
| 74 | 41 | 154 | | |

### Bowling

| O | M | Runs | Wkts | Av |
|---|---|---|---|---|
| 642 | 119 | 2365 | 44 | 53.75 |
| **5wI** | **10wM** | | | |
| 1 | - | | | |

### Best Performances
217 *v.* Warwickshire, Birmingham, 1987
5/69 *v.* Sussex, Southampton, 1988

Chris Smith was one of the most consistent batsmen in English cricket in the 1980s. Equally adept at the top or in the middle of the order, only four Hampshire batsmen have scored more than his 41 centuries for the county and only Mead and Richards scored their runs at a higher average than his 45.63. He was a key figure in the powerful side led by Mark Nicholas.

Having spent the previous summer playing cricket in Wales, including one game for Glamorgan, the Natal middle-order batsman joined Hampshire in 1980 as an overseas player. Hampshire's top order was very fragile and 'Kippy' Smith, promoted to open, was the only batsman to pass a thousand runs, scoring 130 *v.* Kent in his third Championship game and 2 other centuries. Opportunities were limited in the next two years but he came fully into his own in 1983 averaging over 60, the highlight being an innings of 163 *v.* Essex as Hampshire successfully pursued a target of 410. By now English by qualification (the Smith brothers' grandparents were British by

birth), he forced his way into the Test side by weight of runs. Against New Zealand at Lord's he suffered the rare and unenviable experience of being out to his first ball in Test cricket. He kept his place for the winter tour of Pakistan and New Zealand, scoring 91 in 459 minutes at Auckland as England earned a draw. He was one of *Wisden's* Five Cricketers of the Year in 1984 and the world seemed to be at his feet. But in fact, Smith played only one more Test, *v.* India in 1986. His Test career was a typical example of selectorial capriciousness. Most Hampshire supporters would agree that he was a much better player after 1983. Admittedly, he had a difficult time in 1984; starting the season strongly, he finished with an average of 28. But from 1985 he was a prolific run-scorer in all forms of cricket. His most productive season with the bat in first-class cricket was 1985, when he scored exactly 2,000 runs with 7 centuries and 10 fifties. He averaged at least 45 in every season from 1985 to 1991 and can be considered unlucky not to have represented England more often – indeed if he had gone to Australia in 1990/91, not only would England probably have had a more consistent top order, but his younger brother Robin might well have had a more successful tour.

While demonstrating less panache and ebullience, at least on the field, than his younger brother and perhaps blessed with less

Chris Smith – an ever-popular with Hampshire fans.

natural talent, Smith had a sound method and a pleasing array of strokes. Though very orthodox and capable of great concentration, he was normally no slouch. When he and Paul Terry put on Hampshire's record opening-stand of 347 v. Warwickshire in 1987, Smith reached his double century in 309 minutes, only 6 minutes longer than it took Terry to reach his hundred.

He was also a very fine one-day player, again usually going in first. With Terry he holds the record for the highest opening partnership in the Benson & Hedges Cup, 252 v. the Combined Universities in 1990. Only brother Robin and Graham Gooch have scored more centuries than his 7 in the 60-over competition. Especially memorable were his 114 v. Middlesex in the semi-final in 1989 – completed with a broken thumb – which narrowly failed to bring

Hampshire victory and his 106 v. Essex in the second round in 1990 when Hampshire pursued a target of 307. He and Terry put on 173 for the first wicket and Hampshire won by virtue of scoring 307 and losing fewer wickets.

Smith still seemed to be at the height of his powers in 1991 and he scored 1,553 runs in 16 first-class matches at an average of 64.70, with 2 centuries in the match v. Sussex at Hove. He and Terry put on 274 in the first innings and 129 in the second. The two of them were key figures in Hampshire's successful campaign for the NatWest Trophy, but in July he suddenly announced his impending retirement, at the age of thirty-two, to take up a managerial post with the Western Australian Cricket Association. In mid-August – not long before the NatWest final – that retirement became immediate.

# Robin Smith

RHB, OB, 1982 to date

**Born:** 13 September 1963, Durban, South Africa

### Batting

| M | I | NO | Runs | Av |
|---|---|----|------|-----|
| 297 | 495 | 58 | 18462 | 42.24 |
| **50** | **100** | **ct/st** | | |
| 78 | 49 | 157 | | |

### Bowling

| O | M | Runs | Wkts | Av |
|---|---|------|------|-----|
| 168.2 | 22 | 932 | 14 | 66.57 |
| **5wI** | **10wM** | | | |
| - | - | | | |

### Best Performances

209 v. Essex, Southend, 1987
2/11 v. Surrey, Southampton, 1985

Of the three outstanding personalities of Hampshire cricket in the last twenty years – Malcolm Marshall, Mark Nicholas and Robin Smith ('The Judge') – the latter has arguably been the most influential, the disappointments of 2002 notwithstanding. Succeeding to the captaincy in 1998, he had no great tactical acumen but leading by example he took the side to sixth in the Championship that year and into the top nine of the last undivided Championship in 1999, thus ensuring that they were in Division One in 2000. He was then instrumental in securing the services of one of the world's most famous and gifted cricketers, Shane Warne. Neither Warne nor Smith could prevent relegation in 2000 but the county bounced back in 2001, Smith providing a huge psychological boost with an early, dogged match-saving century v. Warwickshire – his first in the Championship since 1998. One of the crowning moments of the season was the county's thrilling win over the apparently invincible Australians before capacity crowds at the magnificent Rose Bowl. Smith rolled back the years to score an inspiring hundred packed with trademark shots – an innings to savour for him and his numerous admirers.

Solidly built and immensely strong in the shoulders and forearms, Robin Smith has spent the best part of twenty years (he scored 3 hundreds in his 7 games for the county in 1983) at the top of the tree as a forcing right-handed batsman. He plays shots all round the wicket, but his particular strengths have been his courage and commitment in the face of the fastest bowling and his rasping off-side shots, particularly square of the wicket. Few men in cricket history have played the square cut with the sheer venom of Robin Smith.

Smith made occasional appearances in 1983 and 1984, which heightened public anticipation as to how he would perform once he was qualified as an England player. He did not disappoint. Against Essex in 1987, he made a magnificent 209 not out, still his highest score, coming in when Hampshire were 5 for 3. He was knocking at the door of the England side for a considerable time and when finally selected in 1988 he at once revealed his quality against the fearsome West Indian pace attack. He was England's best batsman in the Ashes campaign of 1989 and he shone against the West Indies again in 1991.

Smith's Test average of 43.67 is higher than that of any England batsman who has played since 1988, apart from David Gower – higher than Gooch, Atherton, Stewart, Thorpe and

the rest. Smith's exclusion from the England set-up after the 1996 World Cup was, in its way, as witless and vindictive as the earlier omission of Gower.

Smith's international career was not without its problems. Difficulties against Warne in 1993 suggested that he was fallible against high-class spin – although he had made runs against Mushtaq Ahmed of Pakistan the previous year and spin bowling was meat and drink to him in county cricket. More telling, perhaps, was the feeling that – extraordinary though it might seem for such a physically courageous batsman and gregarious individual – he sometimes lacked self-confidence.

He performed better for England at home – only 2 of his 9 Test hundreds were scored abroad. In some ways, his most disappointing tour was that to the West Indies in 1993/1994, when he was the senior batsman. Although he made his highest score in the final game in Antigua, in the early tone-setting games he had not quite lived up to the considerable expectations.

Smith has been an outstanding one-day player. He guided Hampshire to victory in the finals of the Benson & Hedges Cup in 1988 and the NatWest Trophy in 1991, winning the gold medal in the latter as he did in the Benson & Hedges final in 1992. He has scored more hundreds (8) than anyone else in the senior knock-out competition and scored more runs and won more match awards in it than anyone except Graham Gooch. He had an outstanding year when Hampshire won the Sunday League in 1986. A tumultuous innings of 167 not out off 163 balls, with 17 fours and 3 sixes, *v*. Australia (who were playing minus Warne), in 1993 remains one of the most memorable as well as the biggest innings played for England in a one-day international.

Even when he was a leading England player, Robin Smith never gave less than his best to Hampshire. Every year from 1983 to 1997 (apart from 1992), he averaged at least 41 for the county and in four of those years he averaged 56 or more. He may no longer be quite the force he was with the bat but few modern players have emulated Smith's achievement in being an outstanding international and county player, a great entertainer, and being genuinely liked and respected by players and spectators alike.

# Tom Soar

RHB, RFM, 1895-1904

**Born:** 3 September 1865, Whitemoor, Notts
**Died:** 17 May 1939, Llandovery,
  Carmarthenshire

### Batting

| M | I | NO | Runs | Av |
|---|---|----|------|----|
| 101 | 173 | 29 | 1927 | 13.38 |
| 50 | 100 | ct/st | | |
| 5 | - | 49 | | |

### Bowling

| O | M | Runs | Wkts | Av |
|---|---|------|------|----|
| 2770 | 835 | 7697 | 323 | 23.82 |
| 5wI | 10wM | | | |
| 23 | 7 | | | |

### Best Performances
95 v. Somerset, Taunton, 1899

Tom Soar was born at Whitemoor, Nottinghamshire, but failing to make his way in his home county, joined Hampshire in 1887 as groundsman. The club built him a cottage on the ground and provided him with a donkey, a mowing machine, and a boy. By the next season, he was conspicuous as a player as well, capturing 62 wickets for 14 runs each with fairly fast right-arm bowling. His great triumph came in the season of 1895, Hampshire's first in the County Championship, which was one long triumph for him and the stout off-spinner, Harry Baldwin. He had 11 victims for 160 in the first victory in that season of firsts, over Somerset at Taunton, and even better figures in the first home match, and first home win, v. Derbyshire at Southampton, when they bowled unchanged. Soar seized 11 wickets for 113 to Baldwin's 8 for 93. Soar then had the satisfaction of taking 5 MCC wickets at Lord's in mid-June, and he benefited from the fast wickets, and good slip-fielding by A.J.L. Hill and Victor Barton, to take 12 Somerset wickets for 151 at Southampton, followed by 5 for 21 in a totally unexpected victory over Yorkshire at Sheffield. Only three times did Soar fail to take a wicket in an innings. At the end of the Championship season, his total of 89 wickets at 18.60 was second only to Baldwin's 102 at 16.12, and in all matches his victims numbered 95.

Soar remained an invaluable spearhead to the Hampshire attack into the twentieth century, but he had to work far harder for his wickets after that wonderful initial summer, and from 1898 onwards became injury prone and missed many matches. Always a useful bat at 7, 8 or 9, he raised his batting average to 23.62 in 1899. He played the innings of his life v. Somerset at Taunton in July, hitting 15 fours in his 95, and sharing with Major R.M. Poore in a stand of 196 for the fifth wicket. This was, in fact, only the prelude to Poore's partnership of 411 with E.G. Wynyard.

Tom Soar's benefit match v. Essex in 1900 was unfortunately spoiled by rain and brought him little reward. When his career ended in 1904, after a spell as assistant coach at Winchester, he moved to Carmarthen and coached at Llandovery College where he stayed until a few days before his death in 1939. He is remembered as a quiet, introverted sort of man; he encouraged the boys to get to the pitch of the ball, saying 'come dere'. He was employed all the year round, and when the boys played rugby on pitches (which were on the outfield of the cricket pitch), Tom Soar would sit on a box on the square, a lone, dark figure, and make sure that no one set foot on it. The college thought highly of Soar as a groundsman, coach and umpire, and many tributes were paid on his death.

# Edward Mark Sprot

RHB, OB, 1899-1914

**Born:** 4 February 1872, Edinburgh
**Died:** 8 October 1945, Farnham, Surrey

### Batting

| M | I | NO | Runs | Av |
|---|---|-----|-------|-------|
| 267 | 452 | 28 | 12212 | 28.80 |
| **50** | **100** | **ct/st** | | |
| 69 | 13 | 227 | | |

### Bowling

| O | M | Runs | Wkts | Av |
|-----|-----|------|------|-------|
| 507 | 92 | 1856 | 54 | 34.37 |
| **5wI** | **10wM** | | | |
| 1 | - | | | |

### Best Performances
147 *v.* Somerset, Taunton, 1901
5/28 *v.* Sussex, Portsmouth, 1900

Born on 4 February 1872, Edward Mark Sprot rescued a shambles, in spite of the efforts of Charles Robson, when he took over the captaincy of Hampshire in 1903. It took a year or two, but from 1906, Hampshire entered a period of success which extended into the mid-1920s. His captaincy saw the arrival and maturity of Phil Mead, Jack Newman, Alec Kennedy, George Brown and Walter Livsey, of the professionals, and the prime of J.G. Greig, A.C. Johnston, E.I.M. Barrett and A. Jaques. Success was not due simply to the captain, but his power of command and his fine example with the bat and in the field, together with his refusal to accept anything less than the best, welded Hampshire into a successful team which finished fifth in 1912 (the year we beat the Australians for the first time) and sixth in 1914.

He was virtually unknown when he first played for the county in 1898 while still in the Army – he had not found a place in the eleven at Harrow – but in 1900 he scored 857 runs, averaging 26.78, and the following season, in fewer innings, his total rose to 932 and his average 34.51. The 147 he hit *v.* Somerset at Taunton that year remained the highest score of his career. His most successful year was 1905, when he scored 1,206 at 41.58 runs per innings. In 30 innings he was never out for a duck and only three times under double figures. His 141 *v.* Worcestershire included 23 fours; he hit up 110 *v.* Sussex at Hove, and reached over fifty 8 further times. He was as successful in 1907 and 1908. Subsequently, he did not play quite as often – in early summer because, one suspects, he had to care for his ailing wife, who became a chronic invalid – but in 1913 and the following year he was back to his best. In 1914, Sprot, in an innings of 86, and Philip Mead added 149 for the sixth wicket *v.* Kent after five batsmen had fallen for 54, and after five, including Mead, had succumbed to Surrey, he hit up 131 out of an innings total of 239 while numbers 10 and 11 kept up an end. Better still, in 1911, Sprot had pulverised the Gloucester attack at Bristol, his 125 including 4 sixes and 20 fours with he and A.E. Fielder adding 147 for the last wicket in only 40 minutes.

Sprot was famed as a fighter, at his best in a tight place. A very big proportion of his runs came from boundaries – from open-shouldered drives or powerful hits to leg. He also set a fine example in the field. When the 1914-18 war brought cricket and Sprot's period of captaincy to an end, he left Hampshire at a high point and subsequently he fished, drew and painted. His friendship, once given, was never withdrawn; his temper, once finally roused, was formidable and his scorn must have con-

Sprot at home in Farnham, around 1935.

tributed to the prowess of a very fine fielding side. Let it never be forgotten that he won a match by declaring when the county were in arrears and encouraging Phil Mead to take 7 wickets for 18. In returning an autograph book to a collector, he wrote that he felt rather an interloper at seeing his signature among such giants, but in reality he is a giant among Hampshire captains, and his great services should not be forgotten.

# Bob Stephenson
RHB, WKT, 1969-1980

**Born:** 19 November 1942, Derby

**Batting**

| M | I | NO | Runs | Av |
|---|---|---|---|---|
| 263 | 343 | 66 | 4566 | 16.48 |

| 50 | 100 | ct/st | | |
|---|---|---|---|---|
| 9 | 1 | 570/75 | | |

**Bowling**

| O | M | Runs | Wkts | Av |
|---|---|---|---|---|
| 9.1 | 3 | 39 | 0 | - |

| 5wI | 10wM | | | |
|---|---|---|---|---|
| - | - | | | |

**Best Performances**
100* v. Somerset, Taunton, 1976

Bob Stephenson kept wicket for Hampshire during a period when they were as strong as they have ever been and he was also captain for a year, so he has been a considerable part of Hampshire cricket history. His presence – cheerful, unobtrusive but shrewd – was an important element in the achievements of Richard Gilliat's successful side. His contribution to cricket has gone beyond his success as a player – he was one of the earliest activists in the Professional Cricketers' Association – and he has spent his time since retiring from cricket coaching schoolchildren.

Hampshire signed Stephenson from Derbyshire, where he had long been the perpetual understudy to Bob Taylor. Bryan Timms had left to join Warwickshire after the 1968 season and Stephenson fitted in immediately. In 1970 he claimed 80 victims, putting him third on Hampshire's all-time list. In the Championship-winning year of 1973, Hampshire's fielding was recognised as playing a crucial role in their success. Stephenson was equal first with David Bairstow in the national list with 65 Championship victims, including 6 stumpings. The most memorable of those must surely have been that of David Steele (standing up to the medium-pace of Tom Mottram) as he stretched forward in that familiar and apparently secure way in the vital game v. Northamptonshire at Northlands Road.

Stephenson had been first in the list in 1972 and was first again in 1974 and second in 1975,

a clear indication of the pivotal role he played during this successful spell in Hampshire's history.

Stephenson was a useful late middle-order batsman with an unusually, perhaps even uniquely, upright stance. He could defend stubbornly or hit hard as required and he made one century, 100 not out, v. Somerset in 1976. In the final game of 1978 he scored 66 and helped Mike Taylor put on 168 for the eighth wicket v. Glamorgan.

Stephenson spent several seasons as Gilliat's vice-captain and was made captain in 1979. It was a difficult time for the county as the powerful side of the 1970s began to disintegrate – Sainsbury, Richards, Roberts, Herman, Mottram and Gilliat himself had all departed in the last two years while Greenidge and the new young overseas player, Malcolm Marshall, missed several games because of the World Cup; the batsmen apart from Greenidge and to a lesser extent Jesty under-performed and the County really did quite well to come twelfth. Nick Pocock was appointed captain for the following season when Stephenson returned to the ranks and in the second part of 1980, having announced his intention to retire, he was replaced as wicketkeeper by Bobby Parks.

Before moving to Hampshire, Bob Stephenson played soccer for Derby County, Shrewsbury Town and Rochdale, scoring 16 goals in 51 League appearances. His father, George, had played soccer for England.

**Born:** 29 November 1876, Southampton
**Died:** 15 November 1942, Maidenhead

**Batting**

| M | I | NO | Runs | Av |
|---|---|----|------|-----|
| 274 | 468 | 57 | 9167 | 22.30 |

| 50 | 100 | ct/st | | |
|----|-----|-------|---|---|
| 43 | 5 | 361/113 | | |

**Bowling**

| O | M | Runs | Wkts | Av |
|---|---|------|------|-----|
| 12 | 1 | 104 | 1 | 104.00 |

| 5wI | 10wM | | | |
|-----|------|---|---|---|
| - | - | | | |

**Best Performances**
174 v. Sussex, Portsmouth, 1905
1/77 v. Surrey, The Oval, 1909

Hampshire's wicketkeeper from 1902, Jimmy Stone was the first professional from Southampton to become a regular member of the county side. Short and sturdy, he was always steady and competent behind the stumps, but he also had the ability to rise to the challenge of keeping to a more varied and competent attack, as Llewellyn was joined by Badcock, Newman, Kennedy, George Brown and H.C. McDonnell. With the bat, he had been initially regarded as little more than a stubborn defender until he caused surprise by playing a splendid innings of 174 v. Sussex at the United Services Ground, Portsmouth, in 1905.

From that time he was a major contributor to Hampshire's rise in the County Championship through forceful and consistent batting and he went on to achieve 1,000 runs in a season in 1911, 1912 and 1913. 1912 was the season in which C.B. Fry, Phil Mead and A.C. Johnston headed the English first-class batting averages, with E.I.M. Barrett not far behind, and Stone next in line. That year marked the climax of his career as he took a successful benefit v. Yorkshire in the aftermath of the county's famous victory over the

Australians. He went in first and helped Fry put on 109 for the third Hampshire wicket, but following Hampshire's second innings collapse, Yorkshire won the match. In 1914, he lost his place as wicketkeeper to Walter Livsey but played in 13 matches for his batting and hit an undefeated century v. Worcestershire at Dudley.

After eight years absence from first-class cricket, Stone qualified for Glamorgan and filled the gap as wicketkeeper while Sullivan of Surrey was obtaining his residential qualification. After a few appearances for Glamorgan in 1922, he played regularly in the following summer, when he scored 980 runs, average 24.50 – figures as good as in many of his seasons for Hampshire. He must have drawn pleasure from his scores of 37 and 81, which was his highest Championship total of the season, v. Hampshire at Southampton, when *Wisden* described his play as brilliant. His greatest satisfaction, though, must have come from his match-winning century against the West Indians at Cardiff Arms Park. Finally, he was a first-class umpire from 1925 to 1934.

# Mike Taylor
RFM, RHB, 1973-1980

**Born:** 12 November 1942, Amersham, Bucks

**Batting**

| M | I | NO | Runs | Av |
|---|---|---|---|---|
| 145 | 198 | 39 | 3646 | 22.93 |
| **50** | **100** | **ct/st** | | |
| 17 | 2 | 75 | | |

**Bowling**

| O | M | Runs | Wkts | Av |
|---|---|---|---|---|
| 2820.2 | 752 | 7458 | 308 | 24.21 |
| **5wI** | **10wM** | | | |
| 12 | - | | | |

**Best Performances**
103* v. Glamorgan, Southampton, 1978
7/23 v. Nottinghamshire, Basingstoke, 1977

Stockily built and with a ready smile, Mike Taylor was already an experienced and successful county cricketer when he joined Hampshire in 1973, having spent seven years as a capped player with Nottinghamshire. The change proved highly satisfactory for player and county, with Hampshire winning the Championship and Taylor making numerous valuable contributions with bat and ball; Nottinghamshire, meanwhile, came last.

One of six men to appear in all twenty Championship games in that memorable first season, Taylor scored 441 runs at 24 and was, with Bob Herman, the leading wicket-taker, his 63 wickets costing only 19 runs each. He gave an early indication of his all-round usefulness in the first home game, a low-scoring affair in which Hampshire beat Sussex by 7 wickets; he top-scored with 33 not out in Hampshire's first innings and took 4 for 39 in 32 overs of tight, medium pace in Sussex's second innings. In the penultimate game of the season v. Gloucestershire at Bournemouth when the title was secured, Taylor took 7 for 53.

In 1974 his bowling was even more impressive: he took 72 wickets at 17.48, with 6 for 26 (9 for 74 in the match) as Hampshire beat Leicestershire by six wickets.

He started 1975 in fine form before being hit by injury, taking 6 for 32 in a win over Essex and 6 for 26 v. Sussex. In 1977 he scored his first century for Hampshire, 102 v. Essex in a game which Hampshire won by an innings, and took his career best figures, 7 for 23 v. Nottinghamshire (he often seemed to reserve something special for his erstwhile employers), Hampshire winning by 233 runs. 1978 was his best year with the bat: he scored 770 runs at 38 with another hundred in the last game of the season v. Glamorgan, one of Hampshire's four victories that year. He was a consistent performer in the two Sunday League titles in 1975 and 1978.

A neat and orthodox right-handed batsman and an intelligent and accurate medium-paced seam bowler, Mike Taylor, like his twin brother, Derek (Somerset's wicketkeeper for many years), was the sort of cricketer whose career is a compelling argument against the detractors of the county game. Never a serious contender for international honours, he was nonetheless a highly-skilled craftsman who devoted his whole working life to first-class cricket. After retiring in 1980 he became Hampshire's assistant secretary and was subsequently the marketing manager. He finally retired in 2002, ending a thirty-year link with his adopted county.

# Lionel Tennyson
RHB, RFM, 1913-1935

**Born:** 7 November 1889, Westminster, London
**Died:** 6 June 1951, Bexhill-on-Sea, Sussex

**Batting**

| M | I | NO | Runs | Av |
|---|---|----|------|-----|
| 347 | 553 | 20 | 12626 | 23.68 |
| 50 | 100 | ct/st | | |
| 48 | 15 | 127 | | |

**Bowling**

| O | M | Runs | Wkts | Av |
|---|---|------|------|-----|
| - | - | 2375 | 43 | 55.23 |
| 5wI | 10wM | | | |
| - | - | | | |

**Best Performances**
217 v. West Indians, Southampton 1928

Lord Tennyson was a man born after his time. He died in bed in 1951, reading the *Times* and smoking a cigar, by which time the political philosophies of the left had reduced him to articulated rage and he had displaced most of his wealth in the direction of bookmakers, restaurants and wine-merchants.

In some senses the captain that Phil Mead described as a 'big boy' had never grown up, but to suggest that his life was merely a twentieth century rake's progress is to misunderstand a man of enormous energy and physical courage.

He does not seem to have inherited the aesthetic talents of his grandfather, Queen Victoria's Poet Laureate, but from the age of six he demonstrated a capacity to use the cricket bat as a fierce weapon. His father was appointed Governor of South Australia and then Governor General of Australia and in that country Tennyson learned to love horse racing and continued his cricketing education. This developed when he attended Eton and then Cambridge University, but he often featured more as a fast-bowler. In 1909, at the age of twenty, he took a commission in the Coldstream Guards and after some success in Army cricket appeared for the MCC v. Oxford University in 1913 and scored a century on his first-class debut – a feat never achieved by any batsman for Hampshire.

Tennyson's family home on the Isle of Wight qualified him to play for the county and they were not slow to recognise his potential. He made a century in his second match for the county at Leyton, another in the next game at Trent Bridge and then went to Harrogate, where he was dismissed for 96. After half a season he toured South Africa in 1913/14 and made 52 on his Test debut.

No one could sustain such feats through a career and Tennyson's Hampshire career of 347 matches produced 12,626 runs at 23.68. He captained the county from 1919 to 1933, playing on for two more seasons. Occasionally he favoured his early ability with the ball but managed only 43 wickets at a high cost. Although this record appears modest, it masks some rare achievements. He led Hampshire in some of their finest seasons until the 1950s including seventh in 1919, sixth in 1921 and 1922 and seventh again in 1923 and 1926. With a genuinely effective fast-bowler at his disposal that side might have challenged for the title.

Tennyson's self-confidence shines through in this cartoon from the 1920s.

In 1922 he led Hampshire to the most remarkable victory in the whole history of the Championship when they beat Warwickshire by 155 runs after being dismissed for 15 in their first innings. In the previous season he captained England *v*. Australia, and with a badly-injured hand scored 63 and 36 at Leeds. His highest first-class score was 217 for the county *v*. West Indies in 1928 and his Test career average of 31.36 was significantly higher than his county average, suggesting a flair for the big event.

Despite his reckless image, the biggest event in Tennyson's life was almost certainly the years he spent leading British soldiers in the trenches of the First World War. There he displayed extraordinary bravery, in service at the Battles of the Marne, Ypres and the Somme. His brother was killed in 1916, and his mother died later that year while Tennyson was at the front. He moved on to Passchendale and was wounded for the third time in November 1917, which brought his war to a close. He returned to light duties in England only to learn that his brother Aubrey had died in action in the final year of the conflict. The news broke his father, who became a virtual recluse. Despite Tennyson's heroism he was never decorated.

In the context of such experiences it is difficult to make absolute sense of something as relatively unimportant as a cricket career or as shocking as his profligate social life. Suffice to say, that Tennyson was a great man of Hampshire cricket for, as John Arlott observed, 'he was the stuff of which heroes are made.'

**Born:** 14 January 1959, Osnabruck, West
Germany

**Batting**

| M | I | NO | Runs | Av |
|---|---|---|---|---|
| 288 | 486 | 44 | 16134 | 36.50 |
| **50** | **100** | **ct/st** | | |
| 80 | 37 | 328 | | |

**Bowling**

| O | M | Runs | Wkts | Av |
|---|---|---|---|---|
| 5.5 | 5 | 58 | 0 | - |
| **5wl** | **10wM** | | | |
| - | - | | | |

**Best Performances**
190 v. Sri Lankans, Southampton, 1988

Paul Terry came to Hampshire straight from Millfield School and took a while to establish himself. That happened in 1983 when he scored over a thousand runs at an average of 40, batting in the middle order. He began the 1984 season in outstanding form and was the first man eligible to play for England to reach 1,000 runs, hitting a brilliant hundred – his fifth of the season – v. Surrey, whose attack included the ferocious Sylvester Clarke. This convinced the England selectors that Terry was ready to face England's then opponents, Clive Lloyd's all-conquering West Indians. His Test career was brief and traumatic; failing twice in the third Test, he had his left arm broken by the slippery Winston Davis in his first innings of the fourth. The fall of the ninth wicket saw Terry returning to the crease, his arm in a sling, not for the purpose, as in the case of Colin Cowdrey twenty-one years earlier, of ensuring that England did not lose, but with the even more selfless objective of seeing Allan Lamb to his hundred. That goal attained, Terry's innings and, as it turned out, his Test career, was terminated by a Garner yorker.

By this time Terry was an opening batsman in county cricket. In 1987 at Edgbaston, he and Chris Smith put on 347 for the first wicket v. Warwickshire beating the previous Hampshire record of 250 set by Terry and Gordon Greenidge in 1986. Hampshire opening pairs have shared six first-wicket partner-

ships of 250 or more – Terry was involved in all of them, with Greenidge, Smith or Tony Middleton. His most productive season in first-class cricket was 1993, when he scored 1,469 runs at 47.38 including a magnificent 174 at Swansea. The following year he hit five Championship hundreds. He was an outstanding one-day batsman, playing critical innings in the run-ups to Hampshire's Lord's finals in 1988 and 1991, his hundred v. Essex in the 1988 Benson & Hedges semi-final being a brilliant display.

If Terry was a thoroughly good county batsman who was just short of international class, there can be no such reservations about his fielding. Among Hampshire players only Peter Sainsbury and Gordon Greenidge could be put in the same bracket. Terry had an exceptionally safe pair of hands at second slip – in a first-class career of 292 matches he held 332 catches with 1 in each of his Tests – and was versatile enough to be equally good in the outfield, particularly in one-day cricket. He held a record 103 catches in the Sunday League.

In 1996, after the best part of twenty years of loyal service, including several as vice-captain to Mark Nicholas, Terry was suddenly informed that he was surplus to requirements. He took his family off to Western Australia, where he has built a fine reputation for himself as a coach. He has maintained his links with the county and is returning as coach in 2003.

# Bryan Stanley Valentine Timms

RHB, WKT, 1959-1968

**Born:** 17 December 1940, Ropley

**Batting**

| M | I | NO | Runs | Av |
|---|---|----|------|-----|
| 208 | 273 | 67 | 3236 | 15.70 |
| **50** | **100** | **ct/st** | | |
| 7 | 1 | 402/60 | | |

**Best Performances**
120 v. Oxford University, Oxford, 1966

Bryan Timms succeeded Leo Harrison as the county's 'keeper in 1963, after understudying him for four seasons. If Leo was something like a bank manager, all smiles as he ushered a batsman out of his domain, Bryan Timms, neat and dapper, resembled a jockey who had just been successful in his last race and anticipated winning the next. He gave every satisfaction in support of the strongest pace attack for many years, which the county mustered in the 1960s – Derek Shackleton, David White and Bob Cottam. In 1964, his victims numbered 77, 58 caught and 19 stumped, while in the following year they totalled 79 – only six of his victims being taken out of the crease. Leo Harrison, with 76 catches in 1959, is the only Hampshire fielder to have held more catches in a season. In 1964 at Portsmouth, Timms dismissed six Leicestershire batsmen in an innings, four of them caught and two stumped. Altogether, his victims numbered 462 caught and 60 stumped – 522 in all.

He was also a useful bat, good at keeping the score moving along by quick running between the wickets and careful placing of the ball. He never reached three figures in Championship cricket, but hit 120 v. Oxford University in the Parks in 1966. He was also, although few saw him in action, a fine outfield, capable of covering considerable ground, and a safe catch. Bryan Timms was Hampshire born and bred from Ropley, between Winchester and Alton, and was one of the colts reared while Arthur Holt was the county coach. He finished the 1968 season by conceding only 4 byes v. Surrey at the Oval in a match in which both Derek Shackleton and Ken Barrington made their last appearances as regular performers in first-class cricket. As it happened, the match also saw the last of Timms as a Hampshire player. During the winter, he decided to make a break and in 1969, G.R. Stephenson, specially registered from Derbyshire, became the regular 'keeper, while Timms played for a year or two as the reserve 'keeper for Warwickshire.

He retained his Hampshire links and his enthusiasm for the game, and has enjoyed a successful career in business.

# Tim Tremlett

RFM, RHB, 1976-1991

**Born:** 26 July 1956, Wellington, Somerset

**Batting**

| M | I | NO | Runs | Av |
|---|---|-----|------|------|
| 201 | 244 | 65 | 3815 | 21.31 |
| 50 | 100 | ct/st | | |
| 18 | I | 69 | | |

**Bowling**

| O | M | Runs | Wkts | Av |
|---|---|------|------|------|
| 4283.1 | 1235 | 10435 | 445 | 23.44 |
| 5wI | 10wM | | | |
| 11 | - | | | |

**Best Performances**

102* v. Somerset, Taunton, 1985
6/53 v. Somerset, Weston-super-Mare, 1987

The son of a famous father – the greatly respected Maurice, of Somerset and England – (and also known perhaps as the father of a famous son, Hampshire's own promising paceman Chris) 'Trooper' Tim Tremlett was himself a model professional. In the mid-1980s he was a highly-regarded seam bowler, whose career was blighted by chronic injury problems.

Accuracy and control were Tremlett's principal weapons. Operating at just above medium pace, the tall and straight-backed Tremlett could exert a stranglehold over the opposition that made him invaluable in both three-day and one-day cricket. He was very effective at the 'death' in limited-overs games and was Hampshire's leading bowler in the title-winning Sunday League side of 1986 when he took 26 wickets at 18.00.

In the three-day game, 1983 was Tremlett's breakthrough year with the ball. He took 63 first-class wickets at 21.36. He rarely ran through sides, but he rarely gave runs away either and he was always picking up three or four wickets. Usually coming on as first change he would nag away and was utterly reliable, as an outfielder as well as a bowler. In each of 1984, 1985 and 1987 he took over 70 first-class wickets, heading the county's averages in 1984 and 1987 – when he took 72 wickets at 19.54. In 1985, when Hampshire

narrowly failed to win the Championship, he came second to Malcolm Marshall, with 75 first-class wickets at 21.60. He also scored 450 runs at an average of 30 that year. Against Somerset, Tremlett helped Kevan James put on a record 227 in 227 minutes (72 overs) for the eighth wicket, Tremlett making 102 not out with 16 fours.

He had made his debut in 1976 and in limited opportunities in the next few years showed promise as a bowler but played regularly as a batsman in 1980 when Hampshire's top order was desperately fragile. Tremlett scored 717 runs at 27.88, with 7 half centuries. In that summer of numerous different opening pairs, the association between him and Chris Smith was the most successful. Tremlett showed plenty of character, scoring 81 v. Somerset at Bath in mid-June, putting on 174 for the first wicket with Smith as Hampshire reached 300 for the first time that year in a Championship match. Hampshire won just one game, v. Worcestershire – Tremlett scored 76 and 67 not out. In the final game of the season, v. Leicestershire he carried his bat for 70 out of 182 in Hampshire's first innings.

Once fitness problems forced his retirement, Tremlett was a natural choice to manage the coaching regime for the County and as Director of Cricket he is a central figure in Hampshire's future.

# David Turner
LHB, 1966-1989

**Born:** 5 February 1949, Corsham, Wiltshire

### Batting

| M | I | NO | Runs | Av |
|---|---|----|------|-----|
| 416 | 678 | 73 | 18683 | 30.88 |
| **50** | **100** | **ct/st** | | |
| 90 | 27 | 185 | | |

### Bowling

| O | M | Runs | Wkts | Av |
|---|---|------|------|-----|
| 104.2 | 28 | 357 | 9 | 39.66 |
| **5wI** | **10wM** | | | |
| - | - | | | |

### Best Performances
184* v. Gloucestershire, Gloucester, 1987
2/7 v. Glamorgan, Bournemouth, 1981

A pugnacious and resilient left-hander from Wiltshire, David Turner spent twenty-four years as a Hampshire cricketer, longer than any other exclusively post-war player. Indeed, no one else has appeared for the county in twenty-four consecutive summers. He is the only Hampshire player to have been in sides which won the Championship (in 1973), the Sunday League (in 1975, 1978 and 1986) and a Lord's final (the Benson & Hedges Cup in 1988).

Turner was not elegant in the manner of Gower, but he had a distinctive style of batting that was instantly recognisable. Below average height, he had strong wrists and forearms which added punch to his shots, particularly on the off-side. 'An awkward player' was Mike Brearley's assessment, but one who could get runs against top-class opposition.

His first big success came v. Surrey at the Oval late in 1969 when he scored 181 not out, putting on 209 for the third wicket with Richard Gilliat: he was still only twenty years old. Over the next few years the extravagantly sideburned Turner consolidated his position at first wicket down, and he began to be spoken of as an England candidate. Expectations rose after a superb innings of 131 v. the 1972 Australians, Dennis Lillee included. Soon afterwards, however, he suffered a freakish accident, being hit in the eye by a ball from Tony Brown of Gloucestershire – some observers thought that he was never quite the same player again, and he did not manage quite the weight of runs to force his way into the England side.

In the early and mid-1980s, Turner was not always guaranteed a place. 1984 saw a return to regular Championship cricket when Gordon Greenidge was away and he scored 1,365 runs at an average of 41, but in 1985 and 1986 he hardly played three-day cricket. An injury to Robin Smith at the start of the 1987 season gave Turner a fresh opportunity; greyer and moustachioed he responded magnificently, averaging almost 50 and being the sixth highest Englishman in the national averages. Against Gloucestershire he made 184 not out, putting on 311 for the third wicket with Greenidge.

It was appropriate that he was at the wicket when Hampshire beat Derbyshire in the Benson & Hedges Cup final the following year, when he also topped the county's Sunday League batting averages. Turner had become a highly accomplished one-day player – nimble-footed, an expert nudger and nerdler and a brilliant runner. Only Robin Smith has scored more one-day runs for Hampshire.

In his younger days Turner was a superb cover fielder and it was noted in a *Wisden* report of the First Test v. the West Indies in 1973 that his fielding was a feature of the first day's play.

# Shaun Udal

RHB, OB, 1989 to date

**Born:** 18 March 1969, Farnborough, Hants

## Batting

| M | I | NO | Runs | Av |
|---|---|----|------|-----|
| 195 | 277 | 51 | 5172 | 22.88 |
| 50 | 100 | ct/st | | |
| 21 | 1 | 89 | | |

## Bowling

| O | M | Runs | Wkts | Av |
|---|---|------|------|-----|
| 6391 | 1541 | 18581 | 554 | 33.53 |
| 5wI | 10wM | | | |
| 29 | 4 | | | |

## Best Performances

117* *v.* Warwickshire, Southampton, 1997
8/50 *v.* Sussex, Southampton, 1992

Shaun Udal is an accomplished off-spinner who came tantalisingly close to gaining Test recognition. He seemed to be in poll position in 1994 when he was selected for England in one-day internationals against New Zealand and South Africa, where he showed himself to be a skilful and economical operator in that form of the game. In between those two series he was selected in the twelve for the historic First Test against South Africa at Lord's. He had taken 5 for 63 against them at Southampton, including a spell of 3 wickets in 7 balls, but he did not make the final eleven. Although he toured Australia with Atherton's side that winter, the dominance that Australia asserted from the first session of the series meant that it was an improbable forum for the unveiling of a fledgling off-spinner; in any event he suffered injury problems. International honours have eluded Udal since then, apart from a tour of Pakistan with England 'A' in 1995/96. He was mentioned as a possible replacement for Robert Croft to go to India in October 2001, but that place went to Martyn Ball.

A tall man with a longish bouncing approach to the wicket, Udal has been highly effective in county cricket. In 1992, his first full season, he was Hampshire's leading wicket-taker with 58 wickets at a rather expensive 34.68. In the first game of the season he took 8 for 50 as Sussex were bowled out for 149. In 1993, he was again the county's leading wicket-taker with 74 at 30.16, twice taking 10 wickets in a match. No other Hampshire bowler took more than 36.

This steady progress seemed to come to a halt however, after his return from Australia. His performance with the ball in 1995 was respectable but no more and the next three seasons – difficult years for spinners – were very disappointing. 1999 showed a welcome return to form with 50 first-class wickets at 26.72. The 2000 season, however, brought new challenges because Hampshire had another spinner to call upon, namely Shane Warne, and Udal, who was vice-captain, occasionally found himself omitted from the side altogether.

'Shaggy', however, is a resilient character, and he bounced back in 2001 – no longer as vice-captain – to be a key member of the Hampshire attack, taking 54 first-class wickets at 29.81. He was the leading wicket-taker in 2002. By this time he had made himself into a thoroughly useful batsman. Even back in 1993, batting usually at number 9 or 10, he scored over 500 runs at an average of 21. In 1997, he scored a maiden century and he is always difficult to dislodge.

Still only thirty-three, and with a wealth of experience behind him, Shaun Udal still has a great deal to offer Hampshire as they enter a new era.

# Richard Peter Hugh Utley OSB, OBE

RF, RHB, 1927-1928

**Born:** 11 February 1906, Havant, Hants
**Died:** 28 August 1968, Ampleforth, Yorkshire

### Batting

| M | I | NO | Runs | Av |
|---|---|----|------|-----|
| 27 | 34 | 9 | 164 | 6.56 |
| 50 | 100 | ct/st | | |
| - | - | 8 | | |

### Bowling

| O | M | Runs | Wkts | Av |
|---|---|------|------|-----|
| 611.4 | 67 | 2080 | 79 | 26.32 |
| 5wI | 10wM | | | |
| 4 | 1 | | | |

### Best Performances

27 v. Gloucestershire, Southampton, 1928
6/43 v. Warwickshire, Bournemouth, 1928

Peter Utley came as a breath of fresh air when he joined the Hampshire attack in 1927 on leave from the RAF. With Stuart Boyes out of form that year, far too much work was falling on Newman and Kennedy, and no-one else was getting any wickets. In mid-June, a fortnight after his debut, Utley took 6 wickets for 71 v. Essex at Chelmsford, and although achieving nothing else very remarkable, he did well enough to finish third in the averages, with 20 wickets, average 32.05.

The following summer he found time for 17 Championship matches, finishing with 59 wickets, at the cost of 23.27 each, and was effectively at the head of the bowling averages. His best performance was to take 12 Warwickshire wickets for 140 runs at Bournemouth in July. He sent back the Warwickshire opening bat, Norman Kilner, and Len Bates, the number 3, with the third and fourth balls he sent down, and finished with 6 wickets for 43, following with 6 more at the cost of 97 runs in the second innings. Phil Mead played his highest innings of the summer, 180, and Hampshire won by 8 wickets. Earlier, he had taken 6 Middlesex wickets for 70 runs at Lord's, causing the home side, in face of Hampshire's 540, to follow on. He was ineffective in the second innings, when Patsy Hendren played a delightful free-hitting innings of 200, and added 314 for the second wicket with Harry Lee, ensuring that Middlesex more than saved the game.

Hampshire must have hoped that the twenty-two-year-old fast bowler would be a tower of strength for some seasons to come, but he played no more county cricket. The young pilot officer in due course became a monk.

He had been educated at Ampleforth, where he was in the XI from 1922 to 1924 as a most effective fast bowler, who headed the batting averages in the last year. From the age of fourteen he had nursed the desire to become a monk. Ordained as a priest, he entered the Benedictine Order and became a teacher and, later, as Father Peter, a housemaster at Ampleforth. For many years, he commanded the cadet force and ran the cricket in conjunction with the coach, a role filled after the Second World War by his old Hampshire colleague, Stuart Boyes. For his work at the school he was awarded the OBE.

Peter Utley had a beautifully rhythmic run-up and delivery, always bowled a good length, and never tired. He was still bowling well enough to take 5 wickets in an innings in a good-class club match in the last year of his life.

# Clifford Walker
LHB, RM, 1949-1954

**Born:** 26 June 1919, Huddersfield
**Died:** 3 December 1992, Huddersfield

**Batting**

| M | I | NO | Runs | Av |
|---|---|---|---|---|
| 126 | 215 | 32 | 4990 | 27.26 |

| 50 | 100 | ct/st | | |
|---|---|---|---|---|
| 24 | 8 | 88 | | |

**Bowling**

| O | M | Runs | Wkts | Av |
|---|---|---|---|---|
| 978.5 | 274 | 2544 | 51 | 49.88 |

| 5wI | 10wM | | | |
|---|---|---|---|---|
| 2 | - | | | |

**Best Performances**
150* v. Gloucestershire, Bristol, 1953
5/40 v. Combined Services, Portsmouth, 1949

There was some excitement among Hampshire supporters when the county announced that Cliff Walker had joined them for the 1949 season. Born in Huddersfield, he was playing for Windhill in the League when selected to play for Yorkshire v. Hampshire at Bradford in June 1947. Going in to bat when the Yorkshire score had struggled to 55, he drove and hooked well for 91 during a stay of three-and-a-half hours, and he contributed an undefeated 21 in the second innings of a drawn match. A week later at Harrogate, his 65 not out v. the Gentlemen of Ireland was a major feature in their defeat. Gerry Smithson, however, usually occupied the vacant batting slot that year by performances which earned him selection for the MCC tour of the West Indies in the winter of 1947/48, and little was seen of Walker in the following season.

Desmond Eagar, who had been greatly impressed by Walker's early performances, invited him to register for Hampshire for the 1949 season, and he quickly justified the confidence. He hit his maiden century v. Glamorgan at Bournemouth, batting for almost four hours in the second innings to save the match, and adding 138 for the sixth wicket with Derek Shackleton (84). His second hundred of the season again saved the situation, after Hampshire had lost 5 wickets for 50, in reply to Lancashire's 304 for 7 declared. Walker defended well for just over four hours, and Desmond Eagar helped him in a sixth-wicket stand of 101, while with Derek Shackleton he put on 94 for the seventh, enabling Hampshire to obtain a first-innings lead. This innings gave a good indication of Walker's strengths – very strong in defence and a good man to have on your side when backs are to the wall; he was good at the pull and the cut, but not very eye-catching.

In 1953, a very damp summer, only three Hampshire batsmen achieved 1,000 runs – Neville Rogers, Jimmy Gray and Cliff Walker. He began with scores of over 50 in his first two matches, before pulling off another rescue act in the match with Leicestershire at Portsmouth. After 6 Hampshire wickets had fallen for 128, he added 161 for the sixth wicket with Ralph Prouton, and a further 81 with Reg Dare. Ten days later at Bristol, he and Alan Rayment added 246 for the fourth wicket in four hours and fifteen minutes. Walker hit 17 fours in his 150 not out. He shared another big stand (143) for the fourth wicket with Alan Rayment v. Somerset at Taunton. His tally for the season, 1,302 runs at an average of 36.16, stood him at the top of the Hampshire averages.

After a couple of matches early in 1954, Walker dropped out of county cricket. A family bereavement caused him to return north to help in running the family shop. He had hit 1,000 runs in four of his five full seasons at a time when Hampshire were sorely in need of competent batsmen.

# Donald Frederick Walker
### LHB, WKT, 1937-1939

**Born:** 15 August 1912, Wandsworth Common
**Died:** 18 June 1941, flying over Holland

**Batting**

| M | I | NO | Runs | Av |
|---|---|----|------|-----|
| 73 | 126 | 11 | 3004 | 26.12 |
| 50 | 100 | ct/st | | |
| 15 | 4 | 75/1 | | |

**Bowling**

| O | M | Runs | Wkts | Av |
|---|---|------|------|-----|
| 3 | 0 | 22 | 0 | - |
| 5wI | 10wM | | | |
| - | - | | | |

**Best Performances**
147 *v.* Nottinghamshire, Nottingham, 1939

'Hookie' Walker was a rarity among first-class cricketers before the Second World War as he was a public schoolboy who became a professional cricketer. He went to Kings College School, Wimbledon, where, still not sixteen years old, he averaged over 30 in 1928, and he headed the batting averages in the following year. A left-hand batsman, he was a brilliant fielder, who could also keep wicket. He received a trial in Surrey's 2nd XI in 1933, but his home was in Bournemouth, where outstanding performances in club cricket led to appearances for Hampshire Club and Ground, and to his decision to turn professional.

He first played for the county in 1937, and made his mark in his fifth county game in early June, hitting up 123 *v.* Sussex at Portsmouth and sharing in a fifth-wicket stand of 235 with Gerald Hill (161), which remains to this day a Hampshire record for that wicket. By the end of that season he had scored 930 runs, at an average of 25.83, and his place was secure. In 1938, he did not progress as much as was expected due to a succession of minor injuries, but made 925 runs at an average of 23.71, most of them in the number 3 position.

In 1939, he began to move ahead, finishing third in the county averages below Johnnie Arnold and Jim Bailey. For the first time, he reached 1,000 runs (1,149) at an average of 28.72. He hit 3 hundreds at the beginning of the season, and his 107 not out saved the county from defeat by Sussex at Hove. In Hampshire's second innings, in spite of an opening partnership of 149 by McCorkell and Bailey, 5 men were out with 43 of the first innings deficit remaining, but, batting judiciously, he made the game safe; only Walker of the last nine batsmen scored above 25. Against Surrey at Portsmouth, early in August, he scored 108 not out when the next highest score was J.P. Blake's 39 in a match spoiled by rain. Best of all, in a losing cause, was his 147 *v.* Nottinghamshire at Trent Bridge a fortnight later. With Alex Mackenzie (58) he added 157 for the second wicket, Walker hitting 20 fours in a fine innings. Yet, following on 169 behind, Hampshire were put out for only 72. Walker's performances were one of the better features of that last pre-war season.

Sound in defence and with unlimited patience, Walker brought off good strokes all round the wicket, and *Wisden* concluded that he gave every indication of a successful career. Also a strong rugby football player, he captained the Dorset county team and also captained an R.A.F. side.

He had already joined the Royal Air Force Volunteer Reserve at the outbreak of war and rose to the rank of flight lieutenant. He was killed during a flight on the night of 17 June 1941 and was buried in Holland.

**Born:** 13 September 1969, Ferntree Gully

**Batting**

| M | I | NO | Runs | Av |
|---|---|----|------|-----|
| 15 | 22 | 2 | 431 | 21.55 |

| 50 | 100 | ct/st | | |
|----|-----|-------|---|---|
| 3 | - | 14 | | |

**Bowling**

| O | M | Runs | Wkts | Av |
|---|---|------|------|-----|
| 639.4 | 183 | 1620 | 70 | 23.14 |

| 5wI | 10wM | | | |
|-----|------|---|---|---|
| 5 | - | | | |

**Best Performances**
69 *v.* Kent, Portsmouth, 2000
6/34 *v.* Kent, Canterbury, 2000

It may well be that Shane Warne is the greatest cricketer ever to have played for Hampshire – not the greatest Hampshire cricketer, but of all those who ever played for the county, the one who has had the greatest impact on the game as a whole.

Warne has spent one year as Hampshire's overseas player and he is due to return as captain in 2003. That Hampshire's 2000 season turned out to be so hugely, almost traumatically, disappointing, cannot be laid at Warne's door.

The start, admittedly, was not propitious. To bag one pair may be regarded as a misfortune but to bag two, as Warne did in his first two Championship matches, looks like carelessness. Warne was being paid his unprecedentedly high salary because of his incomparable skill as a leg-break bowler and his drawing power as a genuine 'star'. But wickets, too, were elusive in cold, damp conditions at the beginning of the alleged English summer. A hint of his powers was given in a ten-over thrash at the Oval which Hampshire needed to win to qualify for the quarter-final of the Benson & Hedges Cup. Warne bowled two overs and took 2 for 6 as Hampshire won by two runs. In the Championship, his first significant haul came *v.* Durham at Basingstoke – he took 4 for 34 and 4 for 22 as Hampshire gained their first win. He finished with 70 wickets at 23. In the circumstances it was reasonable. He was being asked to win games for a team which exceeded 300 in an innings five times in twenty-nine attempts when he was playing.

His virtuosity as a performer was beyond question. His remarkable accuracy and his mesmerising variations were remarkable to behold – many respected judges felt that the duel, between Rahul Dravid of Kent and Warne at Portsmouth in June, was the most skilful, vibrant and intense cricket seen in a year which included some interesting encounters between England and the West Indies.

Nor was there any doubt about Warne's commitment. Obligations to his national side meant that he had to miss a fortnight in August, coinciding, as luck would have it, with a NatWest semi-final *v.* Warwickshire, which Hampshire duly lost. Warne flew from Sydney to Heathrow and was at once driven to Canterbury to play in a critical Championship match (which Hampshire also lost). He bowled 32 overs on the first day.

Being that rare combination of a star turn and a team player, Warne fitted in perfectly and left with his own credit (if not the club's, at least financially) in better shape than ever. His return is keenly – one might almost say desperately – anticipated.

# Alan Wassell
SLA, LHB, 1957-1966

**Born:** 15 April 1940, Fareham, Hants

## Batting

| M | I | NO | Runs | Av |
|---|---|---|---|---|
| 121 | 158 | 25 | 1207 | 9.07 |
| 50 | 100 | ct/st | | |
| 1 | - | 96 | | |

## Bowling

| O | M | Runs | Wkts | Av |
|---|---|---|---|---|
| 3530.1 | 1359 | 8573 | 317 | 27.04 |
| 5wI | 10wM | | | |
| 11 | 1 | | | |

## Best Performances
61 *v.* Lancashire, Southampton, 1962
7/87 *v.* Surrey, Bournemouth, 1961

At twenty-one, the 'baby' of Colin-Ingleby Mackenzie's 1961 champions, Alan Wassell, a slow left-arm bowler from Gosport, played a significant if largely unsung part in that triumphant campaign.

Wassell had made his debut in 1959, taking 22 wickets in twelve first-class matches. He hardly featured in 1960 and did not play in the early games in 1961 when Mervyn Burden was preferred as the second spinner in support of Peter Sainsbury. But Wassell was selected to play *v.* Glamorgan at Swansea as a third spinner and took 4 for 22 as Glamorgan crashed from 113 for 1 to 183 all out in their second innings. After that, he was more in the side than out. His most memorable performance came in the game *v.* Surrey at Bournemouth when he took 5 for 76 and 7 for 87, 'mesmerising' the Surrey batsmen in the second innings according to *Wisden*; he bowled more than ninety overs in the match.

He had another marathon spell in the critical Derbyshire match at Bournemouth, taking 5 for 132 in 42 overs in Derbyshire's first innings and holding his nerve under a fierce onslaught from Laurie Johnson. He bowled fifty-five overs in Yorkshire's first innings in the last Championship game of the season.

Wassell finished the season with 54 Championship wickets at 24.70. John Arlott, writing shortly after the season finished, thought that he was a potential Test-match bowler and was full of praise for his maturity, control and variety. But it was not to be. In fact, 1961 was probably the highlight of Wassell's career, although he came second to Shackleton in Hampshire's first-class averages with 60 wickets at 27.63 in 1962 and took 70 wickets at 23.74 in 1963: it was only in that year, rather oddly, that he was capped.

By 1964 it was becoming apparent that Hampshire's most potent attack contained the three seamers, Shackleton, White and Cottam, and this meant there was often no space for a second spinner. In 1965, Wassell only played in 12 first-class matches and took 36 wickets at 24.75, although he took five or more in an innings four times, with 6 for 54 *v.* Somerset at Bournemouth being his best effort. However, he dropped out in the course of that season and hardly played in 1966.

Alan Wassell remained a prominent figure in club cricket for many years after he left Hampshire.

**Born:** 14 December 1935, Sutton Coldfield, Birmingham

## Batting

| M | I | NO | Runs | Av |
|---|---|---|---|---|
| 315 | 374 | 101 | 2967 | 10.86 |
| 50 | 100 | ct/st | | |
| 5 | - | 103 | | |

## Bowling

| O | M | Runs | Wkts | Av |
|---|---|---|---|---|
| 9290.4 | 1958 | 25630 | 1097 | 23.36 |
| 5wI | 10wM | | | |
| 56 | 5 | | | |

## Best Performances

58* v. Essex, Portsmouth, 1963
9/44 v. Leicestershire, Portsmouth, 1966

'Butch' White was a big-hearted, broad-shouldered fast-bowler with a long, energetic run-up and a fine action which generated real speed. White could trouble class batsmen by sheer pace. In his heyday, he proved the perfect foil for the metronomic Derek Shackleton.

Fittingly, for a bowler of his type and personality, White's speciality was the devastating burst. In 1961 he interrupted an evening of meandering batting practice by the Sussex middle order at Portsmouth to take four wickets in an over, including a hat-trick – it would have been four in four if a difficult chance had been taken at slip. Hampshire went on to win. In 1962, he got another hat-trick against them at Hove.

In 1965, he took 6 for 10 at Middlesborough as Yorkshire were dismissed for their lowest score of 23. In 1966 White achieved his best innings analysis of 9 for 44, including a spell of 6 for 16 on the second morning when Leicestershire collapsed from 98 for 4 to 135 all out. Three years earlier he had routed the same opposition at Loughborough, taking 7 for 43, the home side being reduced from 50 for 3 to 70 all out in the first innings and 7 for 76 in the second.

White established himself in 1960, taking 124 wickets at 19.10. He also performed prodigiously in 1961, bowling over a thousand overs and taking 117 wickets at 25.39. He also took 100 Championship wickets in 1966 and over 90 in every other year from 1963 to 1969 apart from 1968, when he had 86.

If you had never seen Butch White bowl, you would have known he was a fast-bowler from the way he batted. A left-hander of determinedly agricultural bent whose normal ambition was to hit every ball over mid-wicket, he nevertheless played some important innings, none more so than in a game v. Gloucestershire in 1961, which Hampshire won by 2 wickets: set 199, they were reduced to 162 for 8 but White's 33 not out saw them home with three minutes to spare.

As a genuinely fast bowler with an appetite for hard work it seems strange that David White played no more than twice for England. This may have been connected with the fact that he was no-balled for throwing by the decidedly idiosyncratic Paul Gibb in 1960. Roy Marshall's view was that White's action made throwing a physical impossibility.

White played on until unceremoniously discarded after an injury-hit year in 1971. He played a few one-day games for Glamorgan but he was never going to be one of those bowlers who settle for being a medium-paced trundler. Butch White, like Fred Trueman, was a fast-bowler, through and through.

# Edward George Wynyard
RHB, Lobs, WKT, 1878-1908

**Born:** 1 April 1861, Mussourie, Bengal, India
**Died:** 30 October 1936, Knotty Green,
  Beaconsfield, Bucks

## Batting
| M | I | NO | Runs | Av |
|---|---|----|------|-----|
| 71 | 129 | 4 | 4322 | 34.57 |
| 50 | 100 | ct/st | | |
| 22 | 7 | 89/3 | | |

## Bowling
| O | M | Runs | Wkts | Av |
|---|---|------|------|-----|
| 476.5 | 106 | 1549 | 49 | 31.61 |
| 5wI | 10wM | | | |
| 1 | - | | | |

## Best Performances
268 *v.* Yorkshire, Southampton, 1896
6/63 *v.* Leicestershire, Leicester, 1899

Teddy Wynyard left Charterhouse in 1877, too young to gain a place in their eleven, but compensated in the following season by playing for Hampshire as a seventeen year old against MCC at Lord's. His first appearance at the Oval, in 1883, was in a match made memorable by the high scoring of Surrey, who raced to a total of 650, but Wynyard gave a foretaste of good things to come by top-scoring with 61 in Hampshire's first innings. During four years' tough soldiering in India and Burma, he returned to prove a tower of strength during the County's efforts to regain first-class status. In 1893, his batting average was 50, but he surpassed this the following season when he averaged 66.

The 1894 season was one of frustration for Hampshire supporters. The fixtures of Derbyshire, Essex, Leicestershire and Warwickshire were treated as first class, but Hampshire were excluded. Something special was required from their players and in August the effort was forthcoming – between the 2nd and 28th of the month the County won five matches out of six. Against Derby, Wynyard, in a stand of 127 with H.F. Ward, contributed to victory. He also assisted in the defeat of Warwickshire by two wickets, and he ended Hampshire's campaign with three successive centuries at Southampton – 117 *v.* Sussex, 116 *v.*

Leicestershire, and 108 *v.* Essex. Lord Harris, it is said, added his very considerable authority in support of Hampshire's promotion, which took place in 1895. After that season, Wynyard took over from Russell Bencraft as the County's captain. Under Bencraft, Hampshire finished tenth out of the fourteen counties which then made up the Championship, with Sussex, Notts and Kent of the long-established counties, as well as newcomers Leicestershire, below them. They were initially successful under Wynyard, who led from the front, averaging 50 for his 705 runs; of his 4 centuries, the most remarkable was the 268 which he amassed against the mighty Yorkshire attack at Southampton in July. He batted for six hours, scoring his runs out of a total of 402. At the end, Yorkshire, compelled to follow on, were on 27 runs ahead, and with one man injured had, in effect, only one wicket to fall.

That year, he was selected to play for England *v.* Australia in the third test match at the Oval. He had already scored well against the tourists, with innings of 37 and 68 for Hampshire, and 58 and 4 not out for MCC. The test was played against the background of a rebellion by five players in support of an increase in their test match fee from £10 to £20. Any one of fifteen nominees might have played before the 'strike' collapsed and the final

Teddy Wynyard – a great all-round sportsman.

eleven, which included Wynyard, crystallised. The match was full of incident following rain, which delayed the start until 4.55 p.m. Wynyard contributed 10 to England's first innings total of 145. He claimed that to bat so long in the middle of an England collapse was one of the proudest achievements of his life.

As the 1890s moved on, the County's fortunes slumped as they failed to find support for Baldwin and Soar. Worse still, Wynyard, while nominally captain, was often absent. In 1898, he played only three times, and once was found playing elsewhere in first-class cricket when Hampshire were playing a Championship match! In 1899, he appeared much more frequently, scoring 892 runs, averaging 49, although he played only 19 innings in Championship games. It was in this year that he took part in that memorable stand of 411 *v.* Somerset at Taunton, already described in the biography of Robert Poore.

Wynyard served in the South African War from 1899 to 1902, and after it his appear-ances for Hampshire were few, the last being in 1908. He continued to score heavily for MCC and club sides, as well as touring teams abroad to the West Indies 1904/05, South Africa 1905/06 and 1909/10, New Zealand 1906/07, North America 1907, Egypt 1909, and even after the First World War to the USA and Canada in 1920, and Canada again in 1923 when he captained the Free Foresters – and drove a six over fine leg! C.B. Fry described him as a genius – a batsman who played his strokes extremely hard and the finest fielder in England.

Wynyard was also a member of the Old Carthusian team which won the FA Cup in 1880/1881. He was a skilful player of rugby and hockey, and in 1899 he won the International Toboggan Race at Davos. He married late in life and his son described him as the most gentle and patient of cricket coaches. He must have mellowed – his contemporaries found him impatient and irascible!